YARDS AFTER CONTACT

Team Jack: Scoring a Touchdown Against Childhood Brain Cancer

ANDREW HOFFMAN

Foreword by REX BURKHEAD

Yards After Contact
Team Jack: Scoring a Touchdown
Against Childhood Brain Cancer

Author: Andrew Hoffman

Foreword: Rex Burkhead

Afterword: Michael Nicloy

Contributing Editor: RaeAnne Marie Scargall

Associate Editors: Kylie Dockter, Griffin Mill

Proofreader: Lyda Rose Haerle

Cover Design: Kylie Dockter & Andrew Hoffman

Interior & Cover Layout: Michael Nicloy

All photos courtesy of the Hoffman family,
unless otherwise indicated
Cover photo: John Peterson/Hail Varsity

All proceeds from sales of this book will be used by the Team Jack Foundation, Inc., for childhood brain cancer research funding.

WWW.TEAMJACKFOUNDATION.ORG

Paperback ISBN: 978-1945907654

Hard Cover ISBN: 978-1945907661

Published by
Nico 11 Publishing & Design
Mukwonago, Wisconsin
www.nico11publishing.com

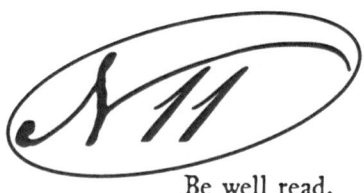

Be well read.

Quantity order requests can be emailed to:
mike@nico11publishing.com

Printed in The United States of America
Standard Printing Co. Omaha, Nebraska

This book is dedicated to my wife, Brianna,
and kids, Jack, Ava and Reese.

Their support was relentless. I am forever grateful for their love.

FOREWORD

By Rex Burkhead

Team Jack Foundation Board Member,
Nebraska Cornhusker, 2009-2012

I was in my junior year at Nebraska in 2011 when I was called into the office of Keith Zimmer, the University's Life Skills Director, and he asked me if I'd like to have lunch with Jack Hoffman and his family. He said the Hoffmans were big-time Husker fans, and that I was Jack's favorite player. That was humbling enough, but then Keith told me about Jack, that he'd been diagnosed with an inoperable brain tumor, and the family didn't know how much time he had left. It was kind of a "Make-a-Wish"-type of a deal, a last wish for Jack to meet some of the players, get a tour of the stadium, and have some lunch. I was definitely on board, and we agreed to meet. That fall, we all met, and I was happy to introduce the Hoffmans to some of the other guys on the team. I gave them a tour of the stadium before we went down on the field and had some races with Jack.

It was a great time. We decided to keep in touch—to see how Jack was doing, how he was progressing, and if anything came up during his treatment.

I was talking with Head Coach Bo Pelini one day and asked him how he felt about inviting Jack and his family out to practice; I thought that might be something cool for them to experience. Coach Pelini agreed without hesitation. Coach really welcomed the Hoffmans with open arms. It was great. Coach Bo is a very kind and thoughtful human being. He just wanted to do whatever he could to help out and get this kid from Nebraska something cool and deserving.

The Hoffmans came out to practice and got to meet the entire team. The team got to learn a little more about Jack and his story. Jack ended up breaking us out of practice that day. He really became a teammate. The coaches were always asking me how Jack was doing and if they could do anything to help Jack and his family. It was really a top down approach, from the coaches all the way to the players. We all accepted Jack as part of our Cornhusker team.

Jack's story was brought to life in our Big Ten home opener that year against Ohio State. The broadcasters did a feature about Jack. A great addition to go along with an outstanding game and performance for our team. At the time it was the biggest comeback in school history.

Fast forward to the Nebraska Football Spring Game in 2013. I got a call late the night before the game from Jeff Jamrog in football operations. He told me the coaches came up with an idea to have Jack Hoffman run a play and score a touchdown during the game. They asked me what I thought about it, and I replied, "If I were him, I'd sure be excited about it. I'd say that's for sure a GO! What kid from Nebraska wouldn't want to do that?!?" We all knew it would be very emotional, which of course, it was.

I had just graduated, so I was standing on the sidelines. I had a view of the play, seeing it develop, seeing Jack come out on the field and get into the huddle with the guys, see them talk through the play with Jack and give him direction on where to go. I had my phone out, recording the whole thing, just trying to get the best view possible.

I've heard people giving Jack a hard time about going the wrong way when he first got the hand off, but if you actually watch it, he's going where no one is. He was doing a great job using his vision as a runner and going to the opening. A proud running back moment, ha.

Taylor Martinez turned him the other way and Jack followed his blockers down the field. The whole time I'm thinking to myself, please don't anybody get in his way, or trip, or get caught up and knock him over. But of course, it ended up being a great moment. He got into the end zone, and the guys were super-excited for him.

It was very emotional. The crowd gave him a standing ovation, and the team carried him off the field. I don't think there was a dry eye in the stands. Everybody knew about Jack and what he was going through at that time, and Team Jack had been spreading awareness of pediatric brain cancer throughout the state of Nebraska. It was a very cool moment. It gained a lot of popularity, passing through television broadcasts all across the country, and then "The Run" won the ESPY for "Moment of the Year." It was pretty awesome.

My parents have also built a strong friendship with the Hoffmans. The family came down to Texas for my wedding, and they've come and visited during our annual event I hold for the Team Jack Foundation in my hometown. They stayed with my parents there. Jack stayed in my old room from when I was a kid. The Hoffmans are definitely like family to the Burkheads. We mesh very well.

I joined the Team Jack Foundation as a member of the board. My skill set in the foundation is spreading the word, using my platform as an NFL player to keep the awareness going, through social media, or any other way I can. Every year, the NFL has one game weekend called "My Cause My Cleats." Players in the league design their cleats with the logo of the charity they support, to raise awareness and funds from the auction of those shoes after the game. I've had the privilege to wear a design on my cleats for Team Jack every season the NFL has done it. My game-worn shoes are then auctioned off through an NFL website, and all the proceeds go to Team Jack. I love being able to do that, as well as spreading the awareness down to my hometown of Plano, Texas. We have a tremendous support team there that has enthusiastically rallied behind the cause. We've held an annual fundraising event for the past few years (including a virtual event in 2020) and have raised over $250,000. That is pretty special for me to get to do that for Team Jack. It's been fun to be a part of that and to have the people I grew up with be a part of it as well. I also am learning more about the science and treatment for pediatric brain cancer and why more money needs to be raised for research. A lot of the treatment options for kids with brain tumors are over 20 years old. To be a part of this foundation that works to bring up newer treatment options for these kids and funds this much-needed research has been truly amazing.

I am proud to call Andy Hoffman my friend. I enjoy our phone calls, whether it's talking about Husker football, or just his being a mentor to me with my annual event or other aspects of life. He became a Boston sports fan, and especially a big Patriots fan, ever since Jack was going out to Boston for his treatments and checkups. So, when I signed with the Patriots, he was definitely on board with that!

We've experienced some big-time moments together. Both joyful and tearful. We've developed a lifelong friendship, and not just around cancer or granting a child's wish. It turned into something beyond that, and it all started with that meeting in Keith Zimmer's office.

INTRODUCTION

This story began on April 22nd, 2011. I will never need a calendar to remind me. The date and what followed are forever etched in my memory. And even beyond the publication of this book, the story continues, unfolding daily. It may not have a happy ending. Only God knows.

There are countless inspirational cancer books. This is not one of them. Several known authors were consulted and asked to co-author this book, but all declined. They claimed the book was "just another cancer story." Whether or not this story is such will be your decision—not theirs. This story will speak for itself.

This is the story of my son, Jack Hoffman, and the cancer foundation named in his honor—one of primarily Nebraska fame. With our being from a small town, we like it that way. While there have been bursts of national exposure, the story told on the pages that follow will hopefully reach most of my fellow Nebraskan Cornhusker football fans. I wrote this book for Nebraskans, my son being one of us.

This story is a glimpse into some of the bewildering things that this little boy from Nebraska experienced and the moments that shook our family to the core and every crack between.

This book is the mission statement for the Team Jack Foundation, a Nebraskan business that tirelessly works daily to improve brain cancer treatment in its region and nationally fund child brain cancer research. I hope you can open this book and know Jack and what his foundation stands for.

Our family is classically Midwestern. I grew up scooping hog manure on a small farm east of Spencer, Nebraska. My wife grew up in the hay fields of south-central South Dakota. Our kids were all born in Nebraska. We live in a small town and work hard, no different than many Americans.

I wrote this book after significant urging from friends, family, and colleagues.

By purchasing this book, you are directly making a real difference. I was not paid to write this book. I will not receive any royalties or payments whatsoever. One hundred percent of the profits from this book will be donated to the Team Jack Foundation. The Foundation holds all printing and publication rights to this manuscript. I do not believe that profiting from a story that was written by God and made possible by generous Nebraskans is ethical.

It is my dream that this story will someday be part of the final and unwritten chapter: the cure.

Chapter One

THE BREAKFAST

The alarm clock blared from the upstairs bedroom. It was 7:05 a.m. on Friday, April 22nd, 2011. The sound didn't faze me. I'd been up embarrassingly late the night before, preparing to have a weekend out of town. All the projects that had waited for weeks had become important and demanded a response. Any workaholic knows exactly what I mean. I'd finally gone to bed just three hours earlier.

Only one workday separated our family from a fun-filled weekend. A Dierks Bentley concert and a waterpark hotel awaited our crew in Sioux Falls, South Dakota, where my wife's sister lived.

I was stuck in a particularly gruesome time with my law practice. I needed a breather from my multi-felony-count, court-appointed client facing two hundred forty years behind bars and twenty-some open divorce files. Pizza, swimming, beer, chips, fun, and a concert were the perfect prescription.

My wife, Brianna, abruptly awakened me.

"Andy, I need you to come downstairs and check on Jack for me…something is wrong," she said with a hint of panic.

"What's wrong?" I mumbled.

"Jack is downstairs at the breakfast table. He's awake, but he's not responding or eating breakfast. It's like he's having a stroke," she explained. "I keep saying his name. It's really weird. He was even acting strangely in the bathroom before coming downstairs."

Mentally, I assumed it was five-year-old-boy stuff and an overly paranoid mom. I hopped out of bed. I was going to fix it; what she said didn't make any sense. We'd watched a movie the night before and he'd been fine.

I hurried downstairs to the kitchen wearing nothing but boxer shorts. Upon my arrival, I saw my son at the breakfast table. Like something out of a horror movie, he sat while intensely grinding his teeth. His hands were at his sides.

I lowered my face to his eyes. Frantically, I tried talking to him. There was no response—just a ghostly stare.

Panic quickly set in. I knelt down, clapped my hands, and yelled, "Jack…Jack…Jack!" Still zero response. He was oblivious. It was an image I would never forget, no matter how hard I tried…my beautiful, healthy little boy, gazing off into the abyss.

"We need to take him to the emergency room," I ordered. "Now!"

As Bri was the only one not in her underwear, she grabbed him and headed for the door.

She threw Jack onto the middle seat of our family suburban. She didn't spare time to buckle him in. As she made the one-mile jaunt through town, she reached back and touched his leg. It comforted her in the minute that felt like an hour. When she arrived at the hospital, she opened the car door, grabbed Jack, and rushed for the entrance. Through his unresponsive fog, Jack somehow hugged her.

Atkinson is a town of twelve hundred people. It is home to no stoplights and a critical-access, seventeen-bed rural hospital. It was the only option at that point. The local physician assistant and the locum tenum doctor were the only emergency room options.

Even that early, I realized that was our unpredictable, terrifying medical reality.

As Bri drove to the hospital, I called Dr. Kari Galyen. She was our neighbor from across the street and family doctor. She was not on call—it was her day off. After I frantically explained what had just happened, she told me she would head to the hospital immediately.

Dr. Kari Galyen and her husband, Dr. Jim, moved to Atkinson, Nebraska in July of 2007 so she could practice primary care medicine at the local clinic. Kari was not responsible for any emergency room calls. She was thirty-two. Her daughter went to preschool with Jack.

Kari was more than a doctor. This was personal.

Once Jack arrived at the hospital, medical staff briefly evaluated him as he sat on the edge of an ER bed. Jack stared through the wall, still entirely unresponsive.

"Let's get an IV started," instructed the physician assistant.

As nurses inserted the one-inch needle into Jack's vein, that little boy who hated needle pokes didn't even flinch. No grimace. Nothing. His stoic, lost gaze continued through what would've normally been intolerable pain.

The evaluation continued as the PA inserted a tongue depressor into Jack's mouth to check his airway. Then there was a sudden *SNAP!* as Jack's teeth cracked the depressor in half. It seemed like he was possessed by the devil.

A CAT scan was ordered. They loaded Jack onto a gurney and wheeled him down the hall to the scan room. As they transferred Jack from the gurney to the CAT scan chamber, it happened.

His legs started shaking uncontrollably. Every muscle in his body twitched and flinched. It was a full-blown grand mal seizure. The kind that can kill.

"Get him back to the emergency room now—he's seizing!" yelled the physician assistant.

Jack was pulled back onto the gurney and hurriedly returned to the emergency room. They administered Ativan to stop Jack's seizing, but it persisted for thirty minutes. Medical staff walked the fine line between giving just the right amounts and kinds of drugs to keep Jack from dying and not damaging his young body. That fine line became thinner by the minute.

Chapter Two

IS THIS THE END?

Once Jack's seizure dissipated, another problem appeared: the early stages of respiratory failure. His own mother, a doctor of pharmacy, understood precisely what was happening to her firstborn child. She helplessly sat and watched.

All she could do was pray. So she prayed.

Back at home, I desperately searched for a babysitter for my two daughters so I could join my wife in the ER. Reese was six months old at the time, and Ava was three. I was helplessly stuck in a spinning kitchen.

After an eternally long short stint, I called Bri.

"What is going on with Jack?" I asked.

"Kari just got here, and she says that she's not sure what is going on," Bri breathed. "But she said that Jack needs to get to Children's Hospital in Omaha as soon as possible." My wife paused. "They are calling for a Life Flight. This is serious."

I went numb.

After about twenty minutes, a babysitter arrived. I then raced to join Bri at the hospital.

When I arrived, I went straight to the ER. I walked into a multitude of nurses, aides, and several doctors.

A panicked tremor rippled through the room.

Crash medicines—epinephrine, specifically—were administered to my son. By that point, doctors in Omaha appeared on screens via telehealth to advise the ER staff.

"Should we intubate…?" Dr. Kari trembled sternly.

"Yes; intubate and then prepare for travel," advised the telehealth physician from four hours away.

Bri then gently grabbed my arm and signaled me to get out of the ER. "Come out into the hallway with me, Andy," she said calmly. "You aren't going to want to watch this."

I didn't listen. I stayed. Those could've been my final moments with Jack.

At the time, I had no idea how difficult intubation was. I later learned that effective intubation of a child in a nationally ranked children's hospital was still very difficult. Vegas odds for intubation in a small rural hospital put us at about one chance in a thousand. Especially in Atkinson. They had never intubated a child in modern history.

One staff member after another tried sticking the intubation probe down Jack's tightly restricted airway. Options dwindled.

Other doctors were called. None were available. No anesthesiologists or nurse anesthetists were available, either.

I had the cell phone number for one of the local Holt County nurse anesthetists, as he had been a client of my firm. He answered in the midst of a surgery in O'Neill, eighteen miles away. He could not leave. He apologized. We were on our own.

A desperate cloud hung over the room. I caressed Jack's arm and face, telling him how much we loved him. I repeatedly whispered into his ear, "Jesus loves you. Jesus loves you. Jesus loves you."

I prayed that his soul had the appropriate nourishment. I began making deals with God. I began saying goodbye to Jack.

Midway through the second intubation attempt, the hospital CEO entered the room. I knew of him and that he'd actually been scheduled for an upcoming intubation training.

"Let's try it again," he said after the second failed attempt.

On the third try, the CEO successfully slid the tube down Jack's airway. The entire room exhaled in relief.

"It's time to get this boy out of here," yelled Dr. Randall. "Do a CT scan for tube placement and then leave. Leave, leave, leave!"

Another attempt at a CT scan began to confirm tube placement but also snap a photo of Jack's brain.

Dr. Randall was an Atkinson landmark. He'd delivered Jack in that same hospital five years previously. Dr. Randall, a distinguished and nearly retired family doctor at the time, was not on ER call. Upon hearing the news, he had immediately come to help. This was Jack—one of his kids. He had delivered half the town.

Around that time, Jack's minister arrived at the doorway of the ER. Jack's entire congregation engaged in a prayer chain. The doctors must not think Jack is going to live if they called in our pastor, I thought.

During that final intubation attempt, Bri had left the hospital to grab our daughters and head to Omaha, which was nearly four hours away. We couldn't all ride in the ambulance. I was to keep her updated by cell.

Before she left, I hugged her. We quietly assured each other that if Jack died, we would be there for each other. We would face it together. We were both resigned to the fact that this was how this day was going to end. And it wasn't even past 9:00 a.m.

Bri returned to the house, loaded our baby girls and their already-packed vacation bags, and headed for Omaha. She feared she'd never see Jack alive again—and she drove like crazy. During the drive, she sang songs and talked to our daughters. She was their rock. She never stopped.

Unbeknownst to her, my brother Mike called in a request with a Nebraska State Patrol friend. Mike requested that the patrol squad leave alone a certain speeding blue SUV. And Bri was never pulled over, even though she drove ninety miles per hour the whole way.

The Life Flight helicopter could not land in Atkinson due to a dense fog. They decided to start transporting Jack via ambulance, hoping that he could be moved onto a chopper wherever the fog lifted.

We raced out of Atkinson, basically right behind Bri. I'd never ridden in an ambulance before. Police officers held back traffic at stoplights to shave seconds—maybe even minutes—off of this life-saving race.

Before we'd gotten into the ambulance, a nurse had handed me a plastic bag holding Jack's clothes from earlier that morning. I had seen this before…when a funeral director had given me a client's clothes after a fatal car wreck.

I told the nurse to throw the plastic bag away. It disgusted me. I learned a year or two later that the bag was eventually given to Bri; she'd been so repulsed by it that she herself threw it away.

Small-town America is a great place to live. Ball games, popcorn, friendly neighbors…and handbag ventilators. For nearly two hours, the ambulance sped eastward as the respiratory therapist used bag-mask ventilation to keep Jack breathing. While an electric ventilator would've been nice, Jack's life relied solely and exclusively upon one person's perfect and consistent hand pumping. The respiratory therapist repeated endlessly, "You're doing good, Jack; keep it up. You're doing great." It comforted me.

About forty-five minutes out of Norfolk, the fog began lifting. The ambulance crew member Jacque Anson contacted dispatch for the Life Flight crew out of North Platte. They were going to pick up Jack in Norfolk, the halfway point between Atkinson and Omaha.

The EMTs drove straight to the Norfolk airport. Chopper paramedics rushed into the ambulance and took over. Remarkably, Jack's grandparents (my mother and father) met us at the airport. They had jumped in the car the moment they'd heard the news.

"ABCs, guys, ABCs…Good job, good job," the flight nurse encouraged the volunteer crew.

A portable electric ventilator, a fifty-thousand dollar machine, was then hooked to Jack's intubation tube. The respiratory therapist had visibly tired fingers and sores wrists.

We loaded into the chopper and prepared for takeoff.

Chapter Three

JACK'S FIRST HELICOPTER RIDE

After the chopper took off, the thick, soupy fog quickly found us. We couldn't see a thing. The pilot didn't know if we could safely fly straight to the hospital, so he set our path instrumentally (IFR) toward Eppley Airfield in Omaha. I knew that most crashes happened when pilots used Instrument Flight Rules, but that was the least of my worries. Part of me, in my clouded desperation, hoped the chopper would go down so that I could join Jack in heaven and not have to see him buried.

Once we reached Eppley, the pilot switched to Visual Flight Rules and headed for the hospital.

Around 11:30 a.m. on Good Friday, we landed at Children's Hospital in Omaha. Jack was still alive. Relief flowed over me. But things were going to get much, much harder before they got easier.

Once we entered the hospital, a kind young nurse came into the ICU and tried to comfort our shell-shocked family. The next person to appear was Dr. N. I immediately sensed his lack of confidence… and he was not at all comforting.

The young nurse immediately asked Dr. N. about an MRI, as Jack was under heavy sedation and had IVs available. Dr. N., after consulting with an on-call neurologist, decided against an MRI.

Privately, the nurse told us that she thought the decision was a huge mistake. She tried convincing Dr. N. one more time, but she was ignored.

An EEG was performed in the afternoon while Jack was still unconscious. Bri and I watched with wide, anxious eyes as a radiology tech stuck electrodes to the exterior of our son's head. Was Jack brain-dead? Would he ever be able to talk again? Would he be in a coma for the rest of his life? So many questions catapulted between our heads and hearts.

The radiology technician reported very early on that there appeared to be good brain wave activity—encouraging. After nearly an hour of testing Jack, the radiology tech said, "Let's try to wake him up."

It was almost 4:30 p.m. The last time we'd seen him conscious had been almost ten hours prior. Even when he'd been extubated before the EEG, he hadn't stirred.

"Jack, Jack! Jack!" the technician hollered at the end of the EEG. A moment passed. Then...

"What!" Jack yelled at the technician.

The tech asked a few more questions. Jack didn't respond. It didn't matter. While we had no idea what the future held, we were elated that our son could recognize his own name.

An hour or two after the EEG, Dr. J, the on-call neurologist came into Jack's room. Hurried to start her Easter weekend, she only gave us a few brief, brash minutes. She told us that this was a one-time seizure, fifty percent of all kids have seizures, and the event was nothing to worry about. She swiftly discounted the entire tragedy while assuring us that we would be home by Sunday or Monday.

We repeatedly inquired about an MRI. We explained what had happened earlier that day, that another doctor had feared it was a brain tumor or encephalitis. She was visibly offended by our "challenging" her decision. In no position to argue, we simply listened. She did not budge.

By dinner on April 22nd, Jack was awake but struggling to eat. He was conscious but still suffering side effects of the seizure. He couldn't yet walk, but he wasn't paralyzed.

That night, I stayed in the ICU with my son. I dug through the internet, searching for any information about the sudden onset of seizures in children. There was an article that linked unexpected seizures to brain tumors. I quickly shrugged that off and closed the browser window. Our son—our incredibly healthy, normal son— didn't have a brain tumor. And a know-it-all pediatric neurologist would send him home in a day or two. He's going to be fine, I assured myself.

The next morning, April 23rd, Jack struggled greatly to just walk. He shuffled around the ICU, unable to balance without our assistance. He would step forward but then teeter, as if he'd had too much to drink. Everyone told us it was normal for the postictal (post-seizure) stage, but by that afternoon, Jack still couldn't move without running into a wall.

Shortly after midnight on April 23rd, Jack was introduced to Dr. M. We again voiced our desire for an MRI and received no concrete response.

The day continued. Jack ate a good breakfast, had lunch, and began feeling a little better. In the early afternoon, we were informed that Jack would be moved to a regular floor before heading home. But—before he moved floors—our son would get an MRI.

A new on-call neurologist had reviewed Jack's chart and ordered an MRI. Unfortunately, general pre-MRI anesthesia wasn't an option because Jack had been eating all day.

The comforting nurse was there and commented, "They should have listened to me yesterday!" She was visibly frustrated with her inferior superiors. Little did we know that delaying the MRI would haunt us for the next thirty days.

In general, Jack had improved between arriving in Omaha and the later decision to do an MRI. The entire medical staff had the same set of facts, but Dr. J. had been the issue. Dr. M., the ICU doctor, and another new gentleman, Dr. F., were the doctors who had ordered the MRI. Dr. N. had been a limp noodle without the grit to question the abrasive on-call neurologist. In fact, weeks later, Dr. N. apologized to me for being so gutless, but he blamed the neurologist.

The MRI did not go well. The machine stopped on a number of occasions due to the anxious, shifting five-year old inside.

Shortly after the MRI, Jack moved to the sixth floor. A very smiley nurse greeted us when we got there. That was the only day we spent with her, but we became very well acquainted. As Jack continued feeling better, he and I found the rec room and enjoyed some video games. For a moment, things felt like they were getting back to normal. The nightmare was almost over…we were coasting downhill. The seizure had been a fluke—only a fluke.

Just a few minutes into our gaming, we were interrupted by the no-longer-smiley nurse. She interrupted softly, "The doctor is coming up to visit with you regarding the MRI."

Suddenly, something didn't feel right. My throat slammed down into my stomach. I was too sick to vomit. Too nervous to speak.

Meanwhile, my and Bri's families began arriving at the hospital to see us. My brother Tony and his kids had just shown up, as well as Jack's Aunt Tiffany, her husband Nate, and their baby Noah. We were all set to have a birthday party for Noah at the hospital that evening. But first we had to talk to a doctor about the MRI.

Upon heading back to Jack's hospital room, I noticed a peculiar man with messy gray hair near the nurses' station. He was surrounded by medical residents, pointing at a computer screen, and motioning at his head. They were talking about Jack. Bri and I were then ushered near him, and he quickly realized we were Jack's parents.

Dr. M. was also present, which confused me—why would an ICU doctor be on the sixth floor? Dr. F. was reviewing the scans with the residents.

Our family sat down. I focused on breathing.

Dr. F. cleared his throat and then spoke.

Jack had a deadly brain virus known as HSV Encephalitis.

On a computer, Dr. F. showed us an enhanced scan of both sides of Jack's brain. Pointing at the screen, he said he doubted it was a tumor because it appeared bilobal. He used the word "lesion" several times. I had never heard the word used in that context before. In her report, the radiologist stated that it was likely HSV Encephalitis, as well. We were told that this was very serious.

The concern in Dr. F.'s voice, eyes, and body language said it all. He was more scared than we were…but we would catch up soon.

The implications were clear: our son would likely die from this. This was just as if not more severe than meningitis.

Shortly after that conversation, Tony came into Jack's room. He did not yet realize the severity of the situation.

I was a mess. I told him that I was very angry, didn't have time to talk, and would explain later.

The plan was then laid out for us: Jack needed a spinal tap immediately so that his cerebrospinal fluid (CSF) could be tested for the virus. Doctors explained that it would take several days to get the results back—but they would begin the HSV treatment immediately, regardless. We later learned that because nearly thirty-two hours had passed since Jack's seizure, which had been the first symptom of the deadly HSV, Jack had no meaningful chance at surviving the disease.

Anger still fills my chest when I think about what happened at Children's Hospital in Omaha.

The doctors outlined the spinal tap procedure. They would insert a six-inch-long needle into Jack's back and draw fluid out of his spinal column. The catch: there would be no sedation or anesthesia because he had been eating all day. Jack was at risk for asphyxia if general anesthesia were attempted. All doctors and nurses we consulted with at that point were irate about the delayed MRI.

Had Jack gone straight into an MRI from the chopper, as originally recommended by the nurse, Jack would've been saved from going through an unthinkably horrible experience…being five years old and wide awake without medicine during a spinal tap.

During the procedure, Bri and I waited outside the door.

It was horrid.

Jack shrieked and screamed like he was being torn apart for nearly an hour. I still tremble when I remember standing outside that door, drowning in tears, while Jack cried out for his mom. The noise was traumatic.

Before, during, and after the procedure, I berated everyone I could find. I should have been locked in a closet. One particular, pompous medical student felt my wrath…I specifically had a very angry discussion with one of the medical students. After tearing into her about the malpractice my son was experiencing, she fervently agreed with me. She repeated, over and over, that I had every reason to be infuriated. She was deeply disturbed by having to witness, let alone participate in, a fully-conscious, no-anesthesia spinal tap of a child. She was on the verge of tears—not due to my anger—but from sympathy for Jack.

She was embarrassed. It just shouldn't have happened at a Children's Hospital.

That should have been our first hint to leave Omaha, but we were slow learners.

At one point during Jack's torment, I went to update our family. The waiting room felt like a funeral home parlor. The air held no hope, no confidence. I told everyone that the doctors thought it was HSV encephalitis.

Tiffany's husband Nate was a hospitalist at Avera McKennan Hospital in Sioux Falls, South Dakota. Nate looked at Tiffany gravely as he inhaled deeply—suggesting that Jack was going to die. Tiffany's response further solidified the point; in a panic, she snapped at Nate, "Don't fucking look at me like that and not say anything! What is that look for!? What are you saying!"

Nate calmly tried to explain the seriousness of Jack's diagnosis. Their conversation further set the stage. Our son was officially fighting for his life.

I returned to where Jack was experiencing that horrific procedure. Following the spinal tap, they returned Jack to the sixth floor. He should have been in ICU, given his fragile and tender state.

Once they took Jack back to his room, another flavor-of-the-day hospitalist and Dr. F. appeared. Dr. F. relayed that although he thought the CSF looked good, they still suspected HSV. Dr. F. then went on to tell us that nobody should visit Jack, as any germ exposure was far too dangerous.

The birthday party ended before it'd even started.

Dr. F. informed us that they would start intravenous Acyclovir treatment that night. I demanded to know the treatment's success rate. Sensing that I needed either encouragement or sedation, the doctors attempted to hide their assumptions regarding Jack's death. I received no real confirmation.

In the next breath, Dr. F. explained, "This disease could make Swiss cheese out of his brain. But only time will tell."

Now—more than ever—Jesus was in control.

Ultimately, we later learned that the medical staff's reluctance to give a positive report that day was because Jack was thirty-six hours past his first HSV encephalitis symptoms; medical journal articles cited successful responses to Aciclovir when it was given within twenty-four hours of the first HSV symptoms. Had Jack gone straight to the MRI the morning prior, he could've been on Aciclovir within six hours of his first symptoms.

That night exhausted us. As Jack lay in his hospital bed, completely drained, I stayed awake to watch him, seriously wondering if he'd wake up the next morning. Eventually, my wife and our daughters retreated to a hotel across the street. I took the first shift of what would be many, many hospital overnights.

Mike, my brother who lived in Omaha, told me that he wanted to stay with me. His big-brother sense told him that I needed his support.

Mike (the do-it-yourself, tough-as-nails former Nebraska football player) also thought his watching over Jack might keep the little boy alive. This was not just about providing company. Mike had a role to play—and he played it well.

Around midnight, I asked the nurses if they could contact Dr. M. from the ICU. At that point, he was the only one I trusted. Dr. M. came to Jack's room to console me. He showed deep concern for Jack, opened up about what had happened, was conciliatory regarding the delayed MRI. It was a heartfelt visit.

Jack trembled periodically throughout the night. Doctors instructed that he not sit up for another eight hours to avoid a terrible headache from the spinal tap.

Every time Jack moved, Mike leapt to his feet to check on his nephew.

I woke on Easter Sunday to the sound of a doctor looking at medical charts just outside Jack's room. It was Sunday, April 24th. Later that morning, a well-known Omaha neurosurgeon, Dr. Jill Sutter, stopped by to speak with me. The doctor agreed with the HSV encephalitis diagnosis, and also noted that if there were a tumor, it could be easily removed. When pressed about how we'd know if there was a tumor, Dr. Sutter replied snidely, "Well, we can go in there right now if you don't want to wait."

To this day, I don't think that Dr. Sutter actually reviewed Jack's MRI. Personally, I think the resident reviewed it and then told Dr. Sutter what it said. I heard "tumor" and "good location" more than once that morning. Days later, Dr. Sutter would be running from those words faster than an Olympic sprinter.

In the days that followed, we stayed with Jack, fervently prayed for his recovery, and awaited test results. We learned there was a five percent chance that HSV-negative test results could actually be positive.

On Tuesday, April 25th, the results arrived. Jack had tested negative for HSV.

My wife and I, along with the doctors, decided to continue the intravenous Acyclovir treatment, regardless of the test results. We couldn't risk our son being part of that five percent.

After that point, a seven-day debate ensued between the hospitalists and infectious disease doctors. None could agree on whether Jack should stay in treatment at Children's Hospital in Omaha or go back to Atkinson to receive in-home care.

Most of the doctors could not get us out of there fast enough—but not because we were troublesome. They simply thought that Jack had recovered incredibly well after being there for five days. But one infectious disease doctor remained adamant that Jack stay in Omaha. We mostly agreed with her, as Jack had been exhibiting other concerning and inexplicable symptoms.

Starting back on April 26th, Jack had begun experiencing daily bouts of nausea. Some of these thirty-second-long episodes were so intense that he'd physically gesture for us to hand him the wastebasket.

We told the entourage of medical staff about Jack's nausea every day for nearly a week. We also informed Dr. F., who later personally witnessed an episode. And he was not the only doctor to see it.

Every doctor simply refused to look into the issue. Most assumed that Jack's body was sensitive to his daily medication cocktail or varying smells. Some of them referred to his nausea as "hospitalitis."

Finally, after about ten days at Children's Hospital and no attention to his nausea, I took it upon myself to dig through an online medical database. At 4:00 a.m. on April 29th, I asked the nurse to bring in an on-call hospitalist to speak with me…because after about six hours of my researching, I'd come to the conclusion that Jack had been suffering partial seizures every day.

It was unbelievable; my child had been seizing right there in front of them, and they'd completely ignored it. And despite my request to the nurse, all doctors refused to come and see me. The nurse kindly said that she would ensure my findings were noted in Jack's chart.

My findings were then communicated on Thursday morning. On Saturday (a whole two days later) the doctors finally read my note and brought in a neurologist to see Jack. The neurologist then determined Jack was experiencing either partial seizures or auras, but in either case, Jack's seizure medications needed increasing.

The med increase helped, so it should have been implemented ten days prior when we'd first told the doctors about Jack's nausea.

Deaf ears.

I found that even though Jack was in a teaching hospital, not much teaching or researching occurred. Rounds seemed like social affairs sprinkled with a pop quiz if a new rotating student were present.

In retrospect, my wife and I were too nice for too long. We became easy to please. As working professionals ourselves, we understood how challenging it could be. We understood that our son was not the only patient. Ninety-five percent of the time, we gave the doctors patience, understanding, compassion, sincerity, and respect. They seemingly deserved that treatment five percent of the time.

The most frustrating thing about our being there from April 22nd until about May 1st was that ongoing debate about Jack either going home or staying there. The infectious disease doctors would give us their opinions, and then the hospitalists would call them "hypochondriacs." The first two weeks were nothing but limbo— until they finally decided that Jack would stay in Omaha a full twenty-one days.

May 15th was to be Jack's last day of intravenous Aciclovir. We eagerly awaited that day. As Jack continued to improve physically, mentally, and emotionally, we grew very optimistic that we'd dodged a bullet. A follow-up MRI and spinal tap were scheduled for May 12th. The goals were a clean MRI and no sign of HSV in Jack's spinal fluid.

All doctors exuded optimism. We did, too.

Chapter Four
TIME TO TURN THE PAGE

W̶e had three weeks of trauma and treatment under our belts. Our family's last day of hell grew nearer. It was the last round of a heavyweight boxing match.

Jack felt great and his partial seizures seemed under control. Doctors and parents alike were just hours away from sharing high fives.

Around noon on May 12th, they wheeled Jack out of his hospital room. We met him down at the presurgical suite, and they prepped him for general anesthesia. My skin crawled as I watched my son inhale the gas and swiftly pass out. It wouldn't be the last time.

During the MRI, Bri and I sat in the hospital's loft coffee shop. Countless hours of constant, pure terror and exhaustion weighed on our shoulders. As we sat together, we decided that Bri would step down from being a pharmacist-in-charge so she could be home with our children. We hadn't seen our four-month-old in three weeks, and our priorities had drastically shifted. No longer driven solely by money, we would put our family before anything else. For the first time ever, we completely discarded societal and peer expectations. There was no crowd to please. God was in charge—we felt it more than ever before.

Later on, a familiar female doctor came to find us in the waiting room. We expected a joyous face, but we received pensively pressed lips.

"Everything went great," she said, clearly trying not to pause. "The needle insertion went well, and we were able to get fluid. The cerebral spinal fluid looked clear."

She failed miserably at trying to downplay her next statement. "The one thing we did notice, however, was that the pressure on his spinal fluid was elevated. It's probably nothing…but it is a small concern."

Slightly panicked (but still clinging to our leaving the hospital with flying colors that day), I pressed for an explanation.

"It could be a lot of different things," the doctor responded. "It could be how he was positioned. It's just hard to tell."

Something smelled.

Bri and I relocated to Jack's hospital room where he would later arrive after waking. When he got there, his head pounded and his back was sore as hell.

Even though we focused on coddling and caring for him, our nerves started getting the better of us.

"What the hell is taking them so long?" I asked Bri.

"Just relax," she breathed. "They're probably just waiting for the neurologist to get over here so he can look at the scans."

After century-long minutes, someone knocked on the door. It was the same MRI physician from the waiting room.

"The neurologist and I would like to visit with you in the conference room," she said.

I smiled at her, attempting to elicit a favorable facial response. She did not reciprocate. My stomach fell to my feet, but we hopped up and walked to the conference room.

The physician wasted no time: "It's not good, you guys. We are really concerned about what we're seeing."

"What do you mean?…What do you see?" I asked.

"The treatment did not work," she stated. "The main lesion on the left temporal lobe of the brain actually grew. We're…we are dealing with a brain tumor."

The neurologist jumped in and rambled through technical detail about what the MRI showed. Even though his tone tried at comfort, every word exiting his mouth paralyzed us further.

In that mere few seconds, emotional entropy flooded our lives again. This day was rapidly making the morning of Jack's seizure feel casual.

"We have contacted neurosurgery to have the on-call neurosurgeon come up and visit with you," the MRI physician said. "They should be up in a little bit to give you their perspective and to discuss next steps."

Somehow my stomach sank deeper than my feet.

This was real. One hour before, we'd been deciding which everyday tasks to do once we got home…but suddenly it felt like we were planning a funeral.

I clumsily reordered my thoughts, mentally poured through the many faces I'd seen in three previous weeks, and said, "We don't want another random on-call doctor. I'd like to see Dr. Sutter."

As we waited for Dr. Sutter to arrive, I had to step out for some air. I grabbed my cell phone. We had family everywhere still wondering about the MRI results. Everyone was about to have a bad evening.

Bri's mom was with our daughters at the hotel across the street. Calling her first seemed like the right thing to do.

I immediately began crying after she answered the phone.

"What's wrong, Andy?" she asked. "What's wrong? Is everything okay?"

It was a poorly timed call; my emotions were unchecked.

"What's wrong with our little boy?!" she begged repeatedly.

"It's not good, Bonnie," I managed to choke out. "The spot got bigger. We just met with his neurologist, and now a neurosurgeon is on the way up." I inhaled. "Jack has a brain tumor."

The next call was to my own mother. A similar conversation ensued, but my emotionally sharp edge was slightly duller.

With both grandmothers notified, the news could then reach the whole family.

Around 5:00 p.m., Dr. Sutter arrived on the hospital's sixth floor. She'd graciously stopped by before heading home after a long day in surgery. She joined the meeting after apparently looking at Jack's MRI.

She explained what she saw, sparing us nothing. She dropped the hammer.

She told us that the tumor was next to Jack's brain stem and cerebral artery, and explained that it was very, very deep, and very, very difficult to get to. She emphasized the word deep. She was the neurosurgeon who'd told us the exact opposite only a few weeks before. Now, all of a sudden, the tumor was in the worst location possible.

Too disturbed to question her new interpretation, we let her continue.

She explained that despite its difficult location, she felt she could reach the tumor and remove all of it. However, such a procedure would require incredible risk. Such a surgery would threaten Jack's optic nerves, brain stem, and cerebral artery.

"The biggest thing that you have to be concerned about is a stroke," Dr. Sutter remarked. "If something happens and we tweak the cerebral artery, it could potentially be fatal."

Sutter then looked at Bri and said: "It's a good thing he's only five and weighs fifty or sixty pounds; you can carry him, if need be."

"Like, carry him until he gets better or for the rest of his life?" Bri questioned.

"Forever."

We then immediately discussed the surgery's logistics. Did we need to do it that night? Did we need to wait a few days? Our minds raced, but everyone hinged on the same goal—we had to get it out.

Considering what we'd been through in the previous three weeks (fighting a deadly brain virus that our son never actually had), the doctors decided we should be discharged and go home to "recharge our batteries." Surgery was scheduled for May 20th—eight days later.

Bri and I had asked the doctors many questions in that conference room, and the next one I posed was just as important: "Doctor, do you think we could take Jack to Disney World next week? He's never been there. It's something we've always wanted to do with him."

She replied, "You know, that is a really good question. And you're not the first person to ask me that. If that's something you've always wanted to do, it makes sense…but I think Jack will have a chance, at some point, to go to Disney World."

Her answer only left more questions. We let them linger.

Over the next two days, I toiled over whether or not Jack was in the right hospital or had the right neurosurgeon. I asked our MRI physician about getting a second opinion, but she only provided us printed documents she'd found online. Documents I'd already read.

If only I'd known then that our son's very first MRI had been misread by the radiologist due to improper image enhancement. Why or how such mistakes were made (and left uncorrected) in any hospital is still beyond me.

I recall a conversation between me and my wife the day before we left the hospital for our "week off." I gently pushed our getting a second opinion from the Boston Children's Hospital. (At that time, they were considered the top neurosurgery hospital in the country.) But ignorantly blinded by our own arrogance, we decided it unnecessary because our state was the best in everything. Again, so we thought.

And that thought was cemented by a half-dozen of my personal physician friends.

Chapter Five

JACK'S PARENTS

Brianna Stiner and I met at a street dance in Bonesteel, South Dakota. It was the summer before our senior year of high school.

She was dating a friend of mine. I was a punk football player, always looking for a fight. A year later, Bri and I began our relationship.

Needless to say, I very willingly chased her around the country until she finally said yes. We married young—I was twenty; she was nineteen. We were still undergraduates at South Dakota State University.

Our personalities are markedly different. I'm an extrovert, energized by being around people. Socializing and throwing Cornhuskers parties is something I've always enjoyed. Bri, being more introverted, has always been fine avoiding parties or meeting new people at events. Conservative with finances and religious about keeping a balanced checkbook, she is my counterbalance. God scored us a home run by bringing us together.

Brianna graduated with a Doctor of Pharmacy degree in 2003. Anxious to move back to my Cornhuskers state, we then relocated to Atkinson, Nebraska. A year later, I rounded off our educations with a law degree from the University of South Dakota by commuting and staying with my brother in Crofton, Nebraska.

We chose to live in Atkinson because it was near our parents. It's sixty miles from Bri's hometown of Burke, South Dakota, and forty from mine—Spencer, Nebraska. Growing up, family was very important to both of us, so we mutually decided in our mid-twenties to forego other career opportunities to remain close to home.

In our early years, we worked hard, played hard, enjoyed traveling, and went to Huskers games. And then, on September 26th, 2005, our lives changed. Jack, our first child, was born.

After thirty-six hours of labor, my wife delivered Jack via C-section in a small, seventeen-bed hospital across the street from our house—the same hospital where he nearly died six years later.

Dr. Randall, the doctor who'd delivered half of Atkinson, was the main delivery physician. Other than a minor scare from Jack's heart rate decreasing during contractions, he was a completely healthy baby boy.

A few years later, our family grew. Our daughter Ava was born in September of 2007, and Reese joined the clan in December of 2010. The girls were both born in Kearney, Nebraska, as Atkinson's hospital had ceased delivering babies.

Even though we both greatly valued family, Bri and I were raised quite differently. Bri's parents were both college graduates and understood the importance of education. They imparted that to Bri, and she was high school valedictorian and graduated at the top of her pharmacy class.

I, on the other hand, was a typical rural Nebraskan kid (whose parents worked the hell out of him), and I sometimes skipped school to help on the farm. Bri's parents prioritized homework far more than mine did.

But despite that, my parents didn't want me to labor as hard as they had. We weren't chained to our textbooks, but my parents were adamant that we go to college and even offered to pay for it. As hardworking Republicans, they could muster the cash flow for our schooling—if we promised to commit. They weren't wealthy by worldly standards, but they were successful in their own right.

While I studied at South Dakota State University, I took a constitutional law course. It was my sophomore year. After I left class one day, Bri picked me up. On the drive home, I told her I was thinking about applying for law school.

She didn't laugh at me. She thought it was a great idea and encouraged me to do it. From that moment forward, that simple conversation and verbal commitment to my wife made me a pre-law student. Her support was a game-changer. That support would be essential later when we began the Team Jack Foundation.

My wife's passion for academic success was contagious. Even though I'd only graduated twelfth of twenty-four students from Spencer-Naper High School, I graduated from the University of South Dakota School of Law with a 3.70 GPA and honors. Hard work, internal drive, and focus later helped me jump start a successful legal career.

They would also help me through something quite different in the future.

Chapter Six

JACK'S ONLY CHOICE

We checked out of the Omaha hospital on Saturday around 4:00 p.m., even though we'd asked for a much earlier discharge. Due to moving all the property we'd accumulated, more guests, and a slow-moving hospital, we were delayed.

The discharge instructions were basic but notably heavy. If ever Jack couldn't control a headache with Tylenol, he had to find an emergency room. If Jack vomited—for any reason at all—emergency room. Both could indicate increased intracranial brain pressure.

Our departure was bittersweet. We were thrilled to get out of a sterile facility and return to our rural lives…but the grim reality, however, was that we'd return seven days later for a life-threatening brain surgery.

We had big plans for when we got home. Easter Sunday had been twenty-two days prior, but our children's Easter baskets remained untouched.

The drive went well—initially. Finally together as a family again, we were free of doctors, nurses, technicians, and the stench of cleaning products. But two hours outside Omaha, the ride quickly became unforgettable.

Jack subtly complained that his head hurt. Mere minutes later, he was nearly in tears, screaming about the pain. Then Jack yelled, "I'm going to puke for real!" This wasn't a nausea bout; it was legitimate heaving.

In the way back of the seven-seat suburban, Jack barfed all over everything—himself, the seat, the floor. He filled every crease and crack.

As if a child puking in the backseat wasn't bad enough, we then realized that his intracranial brain pressure was taking over. Jack needed immediate medical attention. Our minds defaulted to the worst-case scenario: Jack won't make it home.

We immediately turned back toward Norfolk. When we reached the west edge of town, we bolted into the ER at Faith Regional. We'd only been out of a hospital for two hours. We couldn't catch a break.

We spent over two hours dealing with a new hand of cards. All of Jack's grandparents reversed their courses home and came to Norfolk to clean our car and check on their grandson. They were equally devastated by the change in plans.

Jack had been so excited to get home. Instead, he faced an ambulance—or chopper—ride back to Omaha.

After nausea medication, speaking with doctors, and some calming down, it became clear that the car ride had been too overwhelming for Jack. Despite an initial push for an emergency MRI right there in Norfolk, cooler heads prevailed and logic returned.

We eventually arrived home at 2:00 a.m., almost twelve hours after we'd left Omaha. The children stirred when we pulled into the garage.

Bri quickly slipped into the house and hid the Easter baskets. It was the most memorable Easter of all time…and we feared it would be Jack's last.

That night, our first night back home since repeatedly nearly losing our son, my wife and I asked the kids if they wanted to sleep with us. That was not customary in our family. Bri and I were just as excited about it as Jack and Ava. Baby Reese was put in her crib, but our other two ran to their rooms, wrangled massive stuffed animals, and piled onto our bed. Including the giant plush toys, my wife and I had four new residents in our bed that night.

Jack slept between me and his mother; each parent held one of his hands.

Only five days separated us between that night and the moment his skull would be sawed open.

Jack awoke on Sunday, his first full day back home, to a throbbing migraine. He was absolutely miserable.

He went to his friend Drake's birthday party but quickly asked to go home after repeated seizures and the constant headache. By 2:00 p.m., we were on the phone with emergency room doctors in Omaha. We feared we'd have to return much sooner than we wanted.

Dr. F had saved Jack's life by ordering that first MRI; he held a special place in our hearts (and still does). We had his cell number on hand. We had a brief debate over calling a pediatric neurologist on a Sunday or an ambulance. The next week hadn't even begun and it was already long.

In the midst of our discussion, I left the room to self-destruct.

I sobbed. I begged God to give our family just one peaceful week together.

I slowly regained my thoughts, and we called Dr. F.

Once we reached him, Dr. F. calmly yet swiftly advised us to double the dosage of Jack's anti-seizure medication. He believed that the seizures caused Jack's headaches and nausea—not intracranial brain pressure. An hour later, Jack's headache was gone. It never returned.

Monday, Tuesday, and Wednesday…each brought peace:

On Monday, we went to the local hardware store for some household items. We left with a hundred-dollar train set.

On Tuesday, we went fishing on our farm's pond. Jack played in the mud, shot people with his water gun, and ran about like a turkey. He caught bugs, swore like a sailor. It was a blast.

On Wednesday, we did the same.

We did our best to minimize visitors; due to Jack's potentially limited time, we greedily clutched his presence.

On Thursday afternoon, we had to travel back to Omaha. We'd savored what felt like three full days of Christmas, but they were over.

Shortly after lunch, we strapped on our big-boy boots, backed out of the garage, and faced our looming endeavor.

When we arrived in Omaha, our family gathered at Mike and Jacky's house. Every single aunt, uncle, and cousin came. After a cookout, Jack had a water-gun war with his cousins…but anyone present was fair game. Jack drenched everybody, and all were willing victims. This could be their last chance—ever.

Jack had to be at the hospital by 7:00 a.m. the next morning. We spent the night at the Carolyn Scott Rainbow House, the hospital's guest home for patients and their families; we'd grown to know it very well in the previous weeks. The sleeping arrangements were similar to home.

After getting in pajamas and brushing our teeth, we sat in bed with Jack. We needed to go into greater detail about what was going to happen the next morning. We had already gone over the "crazy cells" in his head and why we needed to "get the seizures out." But at that point, we owed him a better explanation.

Bri and I held each of his hands, and we asked him if he knew what was going to happen the next morning.

"I'm going into surgery," he said.

"Do you know what they are going to do, Jack?" I asked.

"Kind of. But not really," he replied.

"Okay, Jack, here's the deal. You know how we talked about those 'crazy cells' earlier in the week?"

"Yeah."

"Well, tomorrow morning, the doctor is going to go in and get those out of there. But you won't feel it, because they are going to give you some sleeping medicine, kind of like they did when you had the MRI."

Jack's response was unforgettable.

"Are they going to cut my head open?" he inquired, slightly smiling. Bri and I appreciated his candor. We could not keep from chuckling.

"Well, Jack, that's exactly what they are going to have to do," I responded.

"Okay, Dad," he said.

And then he was done talking about it. The more we talked, the worse it was going to make it.

My wife and I fell asleep on that night the same way we had all week—each of us clasped one of Jack's hands, our other arms wrapped around him as we fervently prayed to God. On the cusp of that surgery, we prayed so much that we ran out of things to pray about.

For some, praying is the last thing done before falling asleep and the first thing done after waking up. It's as important as breathing or eating.

I held his hand and somehow fell asleep with my doubts.

Chapter Seven

SURGERY HELL

We arrived at Children's Hospital at 6:00 a.m. sharp. It was Friday, May 20th, 2011. Amazingly, our minister from Atkinson met us in the lobby—the same one who'd gathered a praying congregation in the Atkinson hospital waiting room a month ago. It was a comforting yet grim reminder of what was to come.

At about 7:30 a.m., Jack's neurosurgeon slipped into the pre-surgical room to speak with us. Then she hit us with some unexpected news—she and her husband had anniversary plans for the next day (Saturday), so she wouldn't be able to follow-up with Jack after the surgery. She told us we could reschedule the surgery if we wanted to.

Seriously?

We had been emotionally preparing for days, a waiting room full of family, and a prayer chain the size of Texas. She threw this at us immediately before the surgery—not via phone the previous Monday or Tuesday?

She offered glowing reviews of her partners who'd be following up with Jack; we "wouldn't have to worry." I wasn't really listening anymore. We just decided to proceed, despite the sudden lineup change.

This was neurosurgery—not a kickball game.

Around 8:00 a.m., we kissed Jack goodbye and watched the surgical team wheel him down the hall. He smiled back at us, waving. There was no way he understood the gravity of what faced him, thankfully. We would not see our son again until nearly ten hours later.

After seeing Jack go, we returned to a room full of anxious family and friends. As hard as I tried to be stoic, I failed miserably. My face and shirt were quickly drenched.

Half of me still needed convincing that it was real…that my five-year-old was so close to death, having his small head cut open by a stranger. It was too much.

I had never before been so thankful for family—all of the aunts, uncles, and grandparents from our party the night before. They hunkered down with us, in it for the long haul. Then my law partner, some other friends, and our pastor arrived. After we collectively had a good cry, we settled in. Our first order of business: a prayerful devotion.

The gathering held a vast array of emotions. One minute we sobbed. The next moment we laughed at something Mike said. We just had to manage in any way we could.

Worryingly, we received no consistent updates during Jack's surgery. We sat for hours upon hours, waiting and wondering. We got our first update around 11:00 a.m.

"The first incision was about an hour ago," the nurse said. "It's going good. Jack is stable." And then she left as quickly as she'd arrived. She didn't answer any questions; she had to get back to the operating room to aid her fellow skeleton crew.

We sat for another four hours. Prayed. Posted updates to Jack's new CaringBridge webpage. We snacked. Wondered. Then prayed again.

At 3:15 p.m., the nurse returned from the operation, even more abrupt and less friendly than before.

"Dr. Sutter is still working. She will be out in a half hour to visit with you," she said.

"Is she going to be able to get it all out?" I promptly asked.

"She will be out in about thirty minutes to talk to you," she repeated nervously, visibly shaken.

We hesitantly sat back down. Only a few moments later, the neurosurgeon emerged from the hallway. My heart sank; it hadn't been a half hour.

What the hell is going on? I thought.

As the neurosurgeon came in, I noticed her pursed lips and tense, hunched shoulders. We were in for an unfortunate update.

She quickly explained that she hadn't gotten all of the tumor out, and was even unsure how much of the tumor she'd actually extracted.

I exhaled roughly. Jack's tumor was inoperable. I'd never even allowed that to be a consideration before. Even though we knew the tumor was deep and operating would be "tricky," Dr. Sutter had only displayed total confidence before that moment. Even the nurses had exuded similar certainty. But now this.

After some stuttering and mumbling, Dr. Sutter continued: "Right now, Jack is having another MRI done. I am very concerned about his cerebral artery. When I got in there, I couldn't find it." There was a slight sheen of sweat on her forehead. "It should have been right there…It should have been right there! It should have been right there."

She'd gotten lost in the anatomy during the surgery.

Then she explained the tumor's appearance in detail. "It was a very sticky, glittery, rubbery substance. In all my years of neurosurgery, I have never seen anything like it before. It was very difficult to get out of there. I'm very concerned about what kind of tumor it actually is."

The consult was over. The takeaways were beyond discouraging. Dr. Sutter may have sliced Jack's artery—Jack could've been bleeding to death right then and there. The neurosurgeon didn't even know what type of tumor she was operating on.

There had never been any mention of another MRI. It was a hasty decision made after a very difficult surgery. It would be done in an hour.

We were shattered glass. The next hour held even more praying and crying.

One of our fellow prayer warriors that day was Dr. Michelle Krieger. She was an obstetrician from Kearney, Nebraska. Her niece was two months into a fight against leukemia at that time. We had been following her fight and praying for her. We understood each other's pain.

Dr. Krieger had performed her own share of cancer surgeries. After regaining our composure, we turned our attention to her.

Bracing ourselves, we asked her the hard questions: "What do we do with a tumor we can't get out?" "What are the next steps? What are the next steps..."

Dr. Krieger spoke in terms of our army versus the cancer's army.

"We have a better army," she said. "Whether it be chemotherapy or radiation, our army is better. We're stronger. We can beat this."

She offered me the encouragement and hope that I desperately needed. I clung to her words. I found my inner perseverance.

We're going to beat this damn thing.

Unbeknownst to me, the resolve that Bri and I showed in that moment inspired those around us. Months later, I was honored when hearing my brother and best friend recant our strength to others: "There we were, all falling apart, and there was Andy, trying to figure out how the hell they were going to destroy the thing. I have never seen anything like it in my life." Mike had then added, "I remember telling my wife that it was unreal. I truly felt like Jack was going to be okay based on the fight of his family alone. I was so proud of my brother. His attitude comforted all of us."

After our counsel with Michelle, we were all talked out. We needed that hellacious day to end.

Around 5:00 p.m., Dr. Sutter reappeared from the depths of the hospital. She carried herself like an entirely different person; she was smiling.

She informed us that the MRI revealed most of the tumor ("ninety-plus percent") had been removed and Jack's cerebral artery was right where it was supposed to be.

We burst into celebration.

We reached the ICU; apparently Jack had already briefly been awake. The nurses commented on how cute our son had been.

"I heard that," Jack said, lying flat on his back in his bandages.

We did not sleep that night. We kept wide eyes on Jack's vitals instead. That was our strength—being de facto members of Jack's medical team. We were quickly learning that we had to be bold; we were his truest advocates.

In the ICU the next morning, Jack woke up in a bad mood.

"Get this thing out of my pee-pee!" he exclaimed. It was the second time in his short life that he'd experienced the displeasure of a catheter.

One of Jack's favorites, his Uncle Tony, burst into laughter. It was a sound we all sorely needed.

It eased my mind to see Jack was far more concerned about the device in his crotch instead of the fact that he was recovering from major brain surgery.

There was no good way to get a catheter out of a five-year-old boy. It was a "count to three" situation.

Once the staff handled that, Jack's recovery could begin—but he still had to spend three more nights in the hospital.

Amazingly, Jack's recovery went wonderfully. While there were subtle things that seemed different about him, they were only noticeable to me and Bri. Neurologically and physically speaking, he was doing great.

As recovery progressed, questions still remained. Just how much of the tumor was removed, precisely? Would we ever know?

During a follow-up visit in the following days, the neurosurgery team once more confirmed that most of the tumor was gone. The remainder of the tumor was referred to as a "whisk."

We wouldn't find out until much later how fantastically wrong that information was. It was off by one thousand whisks.

On our last day, we visited with Jack's neurosurgeon about pathology results. Due to the tumor's rarity, test results would take a while—up to two weeks. At one point, she sheepishly said: "I have a good guess as to what it might be, but I'm not going to say anything because I've been wrong before in situations like this."

Again: Seriously?

A few days later, without any indication as to what we were dealing with, Jack was discharged from the hospital. We pulled the car around to the hospital entrance and an aide helped us load our son, balloons, and gifts into the vehicle. Half of me was thrilled to get back to Atkinson…but the other half of me found it strange that a child in Jack's condition should be discharged so quickly.

Chapter Eight
A COLD REALITY

No parent ever assumes that they will someday negotiate with God to save their child's life. It's unnatural to do. But sometimes, it is all a person has left.

Following Jack's surgery, Bri and I took turns checking on him during the night. In the morning, the first of us to wake would rush into his room to see if he was still alive. Ignorant of the entire healing process, we didn't know if he could have another seizure or just stop breathing in the middle of the night. We felt like brand new parents all over again.

We would literally high-five each other each morning after confirming he was okay. We'd say a quick thank you to God and then go about our day, grateful Jack would be there with us. But come night time, fear incessantly ate us alive. It went on that way for months.

After Jack went to bed at night, Bri and I would hit our computers, researching and studying brain tumor types, treatment methods, and seizure treatments. While waiting for Jack's pathology report to come back, we fixated on discovering the tumor's type. There were over one hundred twenty kinds to analyze.

One night, I went to bed in tears. Bri woke up, asking me what was wrong.

I breathed, "Bri, based upon everything I read, I think Jack has terminal brain cancer…It sounds like it could be DIPG, or something similar to that."

"Andy, you need to stop doing so much research," she sighed. "You're going to drive yourself crazy."

Despite what she said, our unquenchable thirst for information returned every single night.

On May 31st, we finally received the call from Jack's neurosurgeon. While the news wasn't completely devastating, she did still confirm that it was a cancerous brain tumor—not a cyst or other foreign object.

For the rest of the summer, Jack's seizure episodes persisted. And they got worse.

On one occasion, we got ahold of Jack's neurologist while he was at the College World Series in Omaha. From his seat, he increased Jack's dosage.

We chased Jack's seizures all summer. An episode even cut short his learning to ride a bike. He'd just pushed off the pavement for his first solo flight when it hit.

The seizures haunted us; they were the constant reminder of the inoperable tumor in our son's brain. Through mires of research and trying to get second opinions from other hospitals, it was truly a miserable summer.

The weekend after receiving the pathology report, Bri and I decided we had to do something "normal." We took the family camping in our fifth wheel camper.

Even though camping was our favorite family activity, I barely had the nerves or energy to hook the camper up. It was dangerous for me to move equipment in that mental state. At one point, I just started bawling.

I was still reeling. I couldn't stop the questions constantly flooding my brain. Would Jack graduate from high school? Would he play sports or go to prom?

Two weeks after Jack's surgery, we'd traveled to Omaha to meet with his neurologist, oncologist, and neurosurgeon. We were going to learn what it would really take to win this fight—again, or so we thought.

The neurology appointment covered details around increasing Jack's meds, but we left with no definitive answers.

The next day brought a failure of a neurosurgery appointment. The physician assistant sauntered in, acted like we were dumbasses, but had the audacity to start the meeting by asking, "Now, Jack's tumor was in the parietal lobe, right?"

"No! The temporal!" we exclaimed. It was degrading and disheartening.

Later that day, we met Jack's oncologist for the first time. We gave her the full-court press. She "thought" that the neurosurgeon had been able to remove "over eighty percent" of Jack's tumor…but her precise words were, "She was able to get a good bit of it out." She then highlighted how reputably good Jack's neurosurgeon was with tumor removal.

During this appointment, I asked the oncologist point-blank: "Is Jack terminal?"

"I don't know," she replied. There was something refreshing about her honesty.

We felt deeply unfulfilled after those appointments. More than ever, we thought it time to definitively find second opinions. I wish we'd been aware earlier that other families traveled the entire nation to treat their children for cancer. To us (at that time), Omaha was as big as it got.

Upon returning to my law office after those Omaha appointments, I decided to approach Jack's treatment like one of my personal injury cases. My legal assistant indexed and cataloged medical records and prepared detailed descriptions of past and future events. We tracked the number of seizures on a calendar. When completed, it mirrored a visitation calendar exhibit for a custody trial.

Those things my parents, Bri, and education taught me—hard work, critical thinking, drive—would help us beat the tumor. I gave it all I had.

Back at home, my wife did the same. She fed our children, kept our household functional, and held Jack through seizure after seizure. What a way to live.

While getting a second opinion from a big cancer center is one thing, actually going there for treatment is another. We worried about money, time away from work, and our two other children. Those worries were completely eviscerated one night when it finally occurred to me: what good was anything we were doing or saving if we still lost our son? They could take it all—our land, retirement and bank accounts—but they could not have Jack. To me, it was an epiphany sponsored by God. We had to focus on the highest possible purpose.

During breakfast the next morning, I told Bri that we had to officially take the plunge…we needed to do everything it took. God had prepared us for this moment.

The next week, I contacted our financial advisors and told them to move our retirement accounts into a cash position to either pay for living expenses or Jack's care. We did not want those funds disappearing on us.

We sold our cows. We even put our house up for sale—but soon took it off the market after a showing or two. We had other financial wheels turning, so saving our home seemed more logical.

In the course of that summer, we went from fearfully running from Jack's cancer to barricading our strongholds and sharpening our weapons for war. We would not back down.

While garnering the second opinion, some people tried to offer comfort by saying things like, "Well, that way—no matter what—you can say you did everything for your son and have no regrets." That commentary was painfully short-sighted…We were not worried about clearing our consciences; we were trying to save our son's life.

Ultimately, Bri and I both knew that God was in charge. That meant we had to listen to him…and his messages were being received.

We packaged up all of Jack's medical records and sent them to Dr. Susan Chi, a pediatric neuro-oncolgist. It was time to see what Boston Children's Hospital had to say.

Chapter Nine
BOSTON CALLS

The Monday after the 4th of July, I sat in my office while dealing with a client issue and feeling sick about Jack. My secretary beeped in.

"Andy, Dr. Susan Chi from Dana-Farber Cancer Institute is on the phone," she said with controlled urgency.

It was my first time speaking with Dr. Chi. It was also my first time speaking with a pediatric brain tumor sub-specialist or neuro-oncologist. Little did I know that Dr. Chi was one of only thirty-five in the entire United States. Four of those were at Boston Children's Hospital and the Dana-Farber Cancer Institute.

Dr. Chi was the director of clinical studies at the Harvard-based institution. On that day, she had the pleasure of talking to a neurotic father who desperately wanted to know how long his son had to live.

"So, our brain tumor board had the opportunity to review Jack's case," she began hesitantly. "…And we have a few things to talk with you about."

She paused before continuing. "I know that you were just seeking a neurology and oncology opinion, but we have some thoughts about surgery. The information you sent us stated that you thought the Omaha neurosurgeon removed over eighty percent of the tumor and you didn't want a second opinion on surgery. However… with all due respect to your other surgeon, our neurosurgeon here believes that there is surgical opportunity."

I will never forget the exact spot where I stood in my office when she said that. The hair on the back of my neck stood straight up. I got a lump in my throat. Memories of Jack's previous surgery sprinted through my brain.

"What do you mean, 'surgical opportunity?'" I asked.

"So, we had Dr. Liliana Goumnerova look at Jack's MRI, and she believes that there is substantially more brain tumor that could be removed. Therefore, actually, our recommendation is that you consider a second surgery."

The lump in my throat throbbed. I couldn't still my mind.

"Sorry, what was the name of the neurosurgeon who looked at the case?" I managed.

"Dr. Liliana Goumnerova."

"Can you spell that for me…?" I remarked. After all, I would spend the next several weeks, countless hours, researching who the hell this was.

"She is what we would like to call our 'go-to neurosurgeon' for hard cases like Jack's. We really like her around here, and she does a really good job."

We spoke for a few more minutes about Jack's diagnosis, options, and a plan. Ultimately, it looked like the next step for our family was a trip to Boston.

A few weeks later, we had a follow-up MRI in Omaha before going to Boston. While we were there, Dr. Sutter stopped by to chat. At that time, she told us that the remaining tumor was too deep, and if any neurosurgeon attempted to remove it, Jack would not wake up. She had us convinced, even before we boarded the airplane for Boston, that a second brain surgery was impossible.

At that point, Bri and I had been married nearly twelve years… but we'd only taken two plane trips together. The most recent of those trips had been six years before—and she'd been pregnant with Jack.

We were conservative travelers. We lived in Atkinson for a reason. We enjoyed nonstop flights and a generally sheltered existence. A four-hour drive to Omaha coupled with a four-hour flight was no small feat…especially with a seizing child. But his life depended on it.

Our initial medical visit to Boston Children's Hospital was scheduled for August 15th—two days before Jack's first day of kindergarten. That was the earliest we could get him in. Three doctor visits in total were scheduled: neurology, neuro-oncology, and neurosurgery.

Before leaving for Boston, Bri and I had several serious conversations. Most of our evenings were filled with small debates about another brain surgery.

Bri was steadfast in her position: "I am not interested in another brain tumor surgery. I will go out there and listen, but I am not committing to anything."

The first two appointments at Boston Children's were the easy ones—neuro-oncology and neurology. Both went well. The next day was the biggie: neurosurgery.

The afternoon before the neurosurgery appointment, Bri, Jack, and I took a cab down to Faneuil Hall, Boston's premiere tourist trap. Being normal, everyday tourists felt good.

Dr. Liliana Goumnerova's handshake, smile, and confidence were unlike anything we had ever seen. Her poise spoke as loudly as her voice. For nearly an hour, she explained to us the exact location of Jack's brain tumor and her thoughts on the previous surgery.

While listening intently, a question burned deep inside me. "Can you safely get Jack's brain tumor out?"

"Yes," she stated. "I know exactly what your first neurosurgeon saw, and I know why she stopped…but we can go farther."

"Jack's first surgeon informed us that if someone tried to get more tumor out, Jack would likely die," I replied.

"No, no, no," she assured, shaking her head. "He'll wake up."

We then talked about Jack's seizure problem. We explained the seizures in detail and showed her the calendar. We even showed her a video of an episode.

Immediately, she remarked, "If these seizures are not corrected soon, Jack will not be a functional adult."

"Did you say 'adult'?" Jack's mom asked, smiling.

"Yes. If these seizures persist and are not managed properly, Jack will someday be an invalid."

Bri and I looked at each other, both of us now smiling. That was the first time anyone had ever referred to Jack's adulthood. Up to that point, his physicians had us scheduling his burial even before adolescence.

The visit ended with her encouraging a second surgery; she volunteered herself or someone else with defined expertise and skill in pediatric brain tumors. It was a hard sell. However, she was terribly convincing.

We had a lot to think about…two very strong and very opposing opinions from two neurosurgeons. One said Jack wouldn't make it through, and the other essentially said she could cure him.

We left Boston knowing what we had to do: go home and put it into God's hands through prayer.

Chapter Ten

STARTING KINDERGARTEN WITH A BRAIN TUMOR

The day after Dr. Goumnerova told us she could save Jack, our son started kindergarten in Atkinson. We'd arrived home the night before around 1:00 a.m. Despite his lack of sleep, wild horses couldn't keep him from attending his first day.

As his parents, our day began in earnest; we faced the grueling process of making countless decisions.

Would insurance pay for a second surgery? Where would we stay at in Boston for a second surgery? How long would we be there? How would we get there? How would we get home? Could we afford it—and what would it even cost? What would Jack's other doctors think?

Each night, we debated every detail together. Come bedtime, we prayed for direction and answers. We struggled. Deep down, we both knew the right choice…even though it felt easier to fall back on staying with our neurosurgeon in Nebraska because the alternative seemed so risky. But something would not let us settle on that.

Why couldn't we go to Boston? What the hell were we saving our money for? We were football people. We grew up in a culture where you lineup, go for two, and try to win the game.

It was Labor Day weekend…the third holiday in a row full of nothing but fretting, stewing, worrying, wondering, and praying. Not to mention dealing with Jack's ceaseless seizures, for which he was then taking two different medications in adult-sized dosages.

During a Saturday-evening visit wherein Bri and I weren't fighting about decisions—for once—we simultaneously came to a conclusion: God was at work. We looked into each other's eyes and said, "What are we waiting for? Let's call Dr. Goumnerova and schedule surgery." Jack deserved it.

After speaking with the center in Boston, we decided to have surgery on October 10th, a Monday. The date was the important detail; the other specifics could be worked out later.

With surgery scheduled, it was time to notify Jack's ever-helpful grandparents. We appreciated and loved their presence on our journey.

We called the Hoffman side first. Bri and I explained our moving forward with a second surgery. Their usually boisterous manner turned to complete silence. All they knew about brain surgery was how miserable it was to sit through. Not having had the benefit of sitting through our visit with Dr. Goumnerova, heavy reluctance breathed through the other end of the phone.

Next were Bri's folks. More deafening silence. I distinctly recall hanging up the phone after that second call and realizing all of the grandparents thought we'd lost our minds. They basically only understood that the tumor was inoperable, our first neurosurgeon was "the best," and Jack would die in a second surgery. None of them had tried talking us out of it, but we also hadn't opened the door for any to do so.

As we continued informing more family, the priority became clearer to our relatives: we wanted to sit through one more surgery instead of Jack's funeral.

Over the next few days, we nailed down many more details. We rented a furnished apartment for a thirty-day stint, scheduled all pre-op and post-op visits, negotiated our way into full coverage for Jack's surgery with Blue Cross Blue Shield of Nebraska, purchased five one-way tickets to Boston, and, finally, planned a going-away/pre-surgery/birthday party for Jack.

At work, I hustled to transition as many legal files as possible to my colleagues, which was a never-ending task because we would leave on September 27th and not return until the end of October. I made my secretary my power of attorney so she could get mail, pay bills, and keep my home and office functioning. We made arrangements for Jack's new dog, which the vet would house for thirty days.

Our progress was immense, but it lacked a sense of accomplishment. Every night we lay our heads down, the thought of Jack not coming home alive consumed us. And if he did come home alive, he could be a different kid. What if he didn't recognize us after the surgery? What if he had a stroke?

What could we do for Jack before we left? What could we cross off his bucket list, just in case?

It had to be big.

Chapter Eleven

AMAZING NUMBER 22

One year before the nightmare began, Jack had attended his first Huskers game. He wore a brand new jersey donning number 22. In only Rex Burkhead's second year as a Husker, Adidas thought enough of him to put his jersey out for public purchase. Jack likely owned one of the first ones. Rex was a family favorite, and consequently one of Jack's favorites. Burkhead embodied toughness.

Ordinarily, Huskers football season was a time for optimism, excitement, and enthusiasm. But the year after Jack's first Huskers game, our family could only fixate on Jack's condition and our trip to Boston. Those two things dominated every conversation with family or friends. We became intolerable to be around, and we really wanted that to change.

On a somewhat somber yet fulfilling Sunday afternoon, I drafted an email to the University of Nebraska's Associate Athletic Director for Life Skills, Keith Zimmer. After perusing the UNL Athletics website, he seemed the most appropriate person to reach out to.

My request was simple: I wanted to take Jack to Lincoln for a Huskers game and hopefully get a picture of him with Rex. Nothing more, nothing less.

I drafted the email from my parents' farm near Spencer. Their internet was very spotty. I hit send on the email, but it didn't go through. Frustrated with the service, I shut my laptop and thought, *that was a dumb idea anyway.* I packed my computer into my bag, gathered the kids, and headed back home.

Later that night, I fired up the laptop again. The unimaginable popped up on the screen…Keith Zimmer had responded to the email that had apparently gone through.

Long story short, Mr. Zimmer informed us that game days weren't an option due to player restrictions. But he asked, "How about coming down sometime during the week?"

After adjusting schedules and lobbying Bri, our entire family traveled to Lincoln to meet Rex Burkhead. The school marked Jack's absence as excused without question.

We will never forget how it felt when Rex Burkhead came strolling into the Student Life Complex beneath Memorial Stadium. Through a massive smile, Rex spoke to all of us as if we'd been lifetime friends. After Mr. Zimmer made a short introduction, Rex quickly took over and started his tour. Over the next hour, we saw the locker room, HuskerVision Studio (where Rex would shoot a University-based commercial), weight room, training room, coaches' offices, and Memorial Stadium field.

Rex and Jack even had a footrace on the field. It was an amazing sight. Jack's first steps on Memorial Stadium were shared with a Huskers running back.

Rex told us about his family, why he chose to attend UNL, and his long-distance relationship with his high school sweetheart. He was in no rush and was deeply focused on our time together.

While in the locker room, Rex got his shoulder pads and helmet out and had Jack try them on. It was at that time that Jack gave Rex one of his rubber wristbands. In embossed white Comic Sans print, the band read, "Team Jack—Pray." Every one of our prayer warriors wore one, and then our favorite Cornhusker joined the ranks.

"Thanks, Jack; this is awesome," Rex said as he put the band on his wrist. "I'm gonna wear this on Saturday," he added through a smile, as if Pete Rozelle were his commissioner.

Our visit concluded with lunch at the Nebraska training table. We were introduced to other Huskers and athletes. We were all awestruck—especially Jack.

Euphoria filled the car on the drive home. Jack was pumped. Bri and I were giddy. For the first time since Jack's diagnosis, we thought of something other than brain tumors, doctors, mortality, and cancer treatments. We could only talk about how amazing Rex Burkhead was. Our time with him and his consideration were mind-blowing. He certainly was not a typical college football player.

Two days later, the Huskers hosted the Washington Huskies for a game in Lincoln. Staring at the TV on the Hoffman family farm near Spencer, we eagerly studied every play in search of the wristband.

"There it is, there it is, there it is!" Jack shouted when he got a good look at Rex's wrist.

The next morning, we found a photo in the Lincoln Journal Star that perfectly showed the wristband on Rex's outstretched arm as he celebrated a play. It was a lifetime family highlight. Jack was with him that day as he rushed for a record one hundred fifty-seven yards.

Chapter Twelve

MOVING TO BOSTON

The following week, Jack turned six years old. We worried it would be his last birthday. With his second brain surgery less than two weeks away, we threw a monster birthday bash. Complete with his entire kindergarten class and a pair of rented bounce houses, Jack had the party of a lifetime. Just in case.

The day after Jack's party, our family quickly switched focus onto the next step—moving our family from a small cow town to an apartment in Boston. And it wasn't just any old apartment; it was in Mission Hill, one of the most ethnically diverse neighborhoods in the country.

I'll never forget the feeling when we stepped out of the cab in Boston and saw our new apartment. Our next journey had begun.

We quickly paid the cab driver, rolled our bags into the lobby, and ourselves upstairs. After settling in for a few minutes, I took a quick walk over to the local Stop & Shop and purchased our first Boston family meal—hot dogs and macaroni and cheese, our staple for the next thirty days.

Living in the city was amazing. Completely out of our element and without the distractions of jobs, neighbors, mail, whatever, we could just focus on being together as a family. After all, in our minds, our days with Jack were numbered. Our son would undergo his second life-threatening surgery only ten days after our arrival.

As we cruised through our days together and pre-op appointments, Monday, October 10th rapidly approached. On

Friday, October 7th, we waited for nine family members to arrive. They were traveling to be with us through Jack's seven-hour surgery.

My phone rang. "Hi, Andy—this is Keith Zimmer. Would you have time for Rex to say a few words to Jack and the family?"

"Absolutely," I responded, putting the phone on speaker.

For the next five minutes, we were again mesmerized by the selfless commitment that Rex Burkhead made to our son.

They talked about Boston, what Jack was having for supper. Then Rex told Jack he would pray for him on Monday and try to call again a few days after the surgery. In truth, Rex should have been in meetings, focusing on the upcoming Huskers Big Ten home opener. Instead, he was on the phone with our son. The conversation ended with our children chorusing, "Go Big Red!" Rex loved it. And we loved him.

As family arrived through Saturday, emotions flowed. The imminent surgery gripped us in nervous sickness. Grandma and Grandpa Hoffman and Aunt Julia joined us around 7 p.m.—just in time for the Nebraska-Ohio State game.

Jack was in bed by 9 p.m., but right outside his bedroom door, crazed Huskers fans watched Ohio State take a twenty-eight to seven lead over Nebraska. The room sweated.

I'd watched dozens of Husker games. In fact, I don't think I'd missed a single one in the previous three decades. But as I watched that particular game, it was like I was actually in the stadium…not just physically, but also spiritually. The score hit 21-28, and then the Huskers were within a touchdown. Give it to Rex. Give it to Rex… Give it to Rex, my brain hammered. I could feel something great about to happen. And then it did.

Rex took a swing pass from Taylor Martinez, juked a tackler, and raced for a thirty-yard touchdown. The touchdown blew the doors off Memorial Stadium and the roof off of our apartment in Boston.

The end of the game drew nearer. I kept saying, "Give it to Rex. Give it to Rex." It was like Coach Bo heard me. It was truly unreal;

and I wasn't one to quickly jump to ethereal conclusions. I was in the huddle, and Rex said, "Give me the ball."

And then it happened again. Rex took a toss sweep off left tackle and ran twenty-five yards for the game-winning touchdown. Those two fourth-quarter touchdowns went down in Huskers history.

The room fought tears from the Huskers' underdog victory, and then the waterworks took hold as the ABC commentators started talking about Rex: "Rex Burkhead is a terrific young man…and what's not to like? Jeannine Edwards will now tell you about a little boy fighting cancer who has a special relationship with Rex."

Silence rang through our apartment.

Holy shit.

They were about to talk to over five million people about the little boy in the bedroom next to us.

Jeannine Edwards began speaking. "Before the game tonight, we talked to Rex Burkhead, and he told us about a little boy. His name is Jack Hoffman, and he's out in Boston. On Monday, Jack will undergo yet another surgery for his brain tumor. Jack is a huge Rex Burkhead fan…and Rex told us that he'll be calling little Jack after the surgery."

We couldn't believe what happened next.

Commentator Matt Millen asked millions of viewers to say a prayer for Jack.

He then added, "Well, Jack, you picked a good guy to watch. We'll all be praying for you."

Our entire family gaped at each other and sobbed. Team Jack, the prayer movement, was national. Prayer request delivered.

Immediately after the game, we checked our personal Facebook pages. We were loaded with messages. Jack's CaringBridge page was lighting up, too. Right then, a cousin formed a new Facebook page named "Team Jack." Two years later, that page would have nearly eighty thousand followers.

While we'd received countless messages with well-wishes and prayers, one was particularly meaningful: "Only in Nebraska could a meeting between a college football player and a sick child turn into a national prayer request. So proud to be a Husker."

That summed it up perfectly.

The next day, we still buzzed from the night before. The day flew by, and suddenly it was Monday morning.

It was the second time doctors would cut Jack's head open in less than six months.

Chapter Thirteen

SURGERY...AGAIN

I'd never forget the image of Jack's smile as he was wheeled down the hall to his first brain tumor surgery. This Monday morning felt eerily identical.

The family band joined together again in another waiting room for another surgery. We had a private room to ourselves, which we quickly filled with endless prayers and devotion.

Before we'd joined our exceedingly loving and loyal family (who had traveled a combined ten-thousand miles to be with us), we'd met Dr. Goumnerova in the pre-operating room. The doctor had calmly walked in, confident and smiling. She carried a small wooden box. It looked old and worn.

"What's in the box?" I inquired.

"Oh, this," she responded and opened the antique. "These are my special glasses. I wear these for all of my brain tumor surgeries."

They were more than glasses. They were highly intensified eyewear, which helped her distinguish brain tumor from healthy tissue.

It was at that point I began to feel uneasy. I was low on sleep, and I felt tears coming. Generally, I'm a crier. My wife is stronger. Right before Jack had to wheel down the hall, I lowered my head, choked on a sob, and left it to Bri to take Jack to anesthesia. Dr. Goumnerova followed her to give me space.

Upon reaching our family, we collapsed in their arms. We were so blessed by their carrying us. After exchanging hugs and tears, we sat down and got to business. Before we took to Twitter, Facebook, or Caringbridge, we rapidly turned to the good Lord. Pastor Richard Kothe had prepared Bible verses for us on that special morning. Comfort filled the room. As we read aloud, we brimmed with a resounding confidence and strength. We were ready for battle, thanks to that powerful moment.

Without fail, the nurse liaison provided us an update every hour and thirty minutes. It offered even more comfort.

Update number one: "Surgery has started, and the first incision has been made. Jack's vitals are strong. He's doing just great."

Update number two: "The doctors have arrived at the tumor; they're taking their time while they work."

We felt closer to Jack through the consistent communications.

As morning turned to afternoon, the final update came: "Surgery went really well. But when Dr. Goumnerova comes out, she will only see the parents. It is her policy to only visit with Mom and Dad. Don't be alarmed when she pulls you aside."

Moments later, the beaming doctor appeared, still in full scrubs and a mask. It felt good. So much better than the horror we'd experienced back in May. After congregating with the family for a moment, the three of us went to a private room nearby.

She told us the news. "Surgery went very good. As good as we could've expected," she began. "Jack will no longer be experiencing seizures. I am quite confident of that. As for the tumor, we were able to remove at least ninety-five percent, maybe even all of it. The tumor was in a much more difficult location than I expected. After I got in there, I saw that the tumor was pressing up against the brain stem and also wrapped around Jack's cerebral artery. Once I got to the cerebral artery, I was able to scrape as much of the tumor off of the artery as possible."

I tried to keep up with the deluge of information. The first neurosurgeon hadn't found the cerebral artery; but Dr. Goumnerova had not only found it, she'd even manipulated it.

"Where the cerebral artery goes behind the brain stem, it creates a little nook," she continued. "I could tell that there was some substance left in the nook, but I couldn't get to it without seriously injuring Jack. Because I wasn't sure if it was scar tissue or brain tumor tissue, I played it safe. I am hopeful it was scar tissue. If it is tumor, I am confident that we will be able to take care of it with a different therapy." Her proclamation was thrilling.

She described the amount of removed tumor as "substantial," being the same size as a "large date."

What the hell does she mean by 'date'? I thought. She explained it was the size of a golf ball—and probably larger.

Later that week, I was grocery shopping at Stop & Shop. I ran across a package of dates. Holy cow. Dates are huge. We'd never seen dates back in Atkinson. If Jack had a "large date" removed, did he have any brain left upstairs?

The pathology report later confirmed the measurements of the extracted tumor. It was somewhere between the size of a golf ball and softball. No wonder he'd been seizing.

After surgery, Jack went to ICU. We spent the afternoon watching the nurses administer every test known to man. Levels were frequently checked to prevent infection or other complications. Every doctor who came to check in—urologist, anesthesiologist, intensivist, neurologist—wore a smile and offered congratulations. It was a massive success. We felt on top of the world.

After Bri and I took shifts watching Jack overnight, we prepared for his transfer to a patient room. We knew what was in store; it was time to wean off morphine and move to Tylenol, get walking again, and hopefully get his bowels moving.

We made our way to the eighth floor, which also the neurology floor. It was not an easy place to be. Kids from all over the world, most of them suffering from brain tumors, gathered there for the same shot at life. I often wonder (and shudder) about how many of them are still with us today.

That hospital's floor nurses were very special people. Only a Boston Children's Hospital nurse could get a child to suck down oral medication at 3 a.m. Those gals were good.

On our first night on the eighth floor, I was awakened by a nurse telling me it was time for pain medications. "What is your favorite flavor of popsicle?" she asked Jack. We were surprised.

"Orange," Jack replied.

"Coming right up," she chirped.

Mere moments later, Jack sucked on his medicated popsicle like a margarita in Mexico. Again, did I mention that those nurses were amazing?

On day number two, Jack received an important call. My phone didn't recognize the number.

"Is Jack there? This is Rex," the voice on the other end said. It was our hero from the Nebraska-Ohio State game.

Once again, Rex blew us away.

We informed Rex that Jack was having a tough, tiresome day and may not be able to talk much. Rex understood, and we put the phone on speaker.

We then heard Rex describe—in his own words, without edits or media pressures—what had transpired during Saturday night's game. Rex said that when the Huskers were trailing Ohio State in the third quarter, he'd told his teammates, "Jack's not giving up, so we can't give up, either."

Rex had used Jack as the rally cry to inspire his team's biggest up-from-below victory in history. Jack was too drugged to fully comprehend the gravity of Rex's words, but his dad was not. My life had a lot of highlights, but that one was very near the top. Our hearts were bursting. My love of Jack, Rex, and Husker football melded together in that moment in a way I never thought possible.

Even more remarkable was that Rex's father, Rick Burkhead, called my cell phone later that evening. Our conversation was powerful. Rick explained to me how positively Jack had influenced Rex's life. I argued that he had it backwards. Our talk ended with Rick winning, and I overflowed with gratitude for the Burkhead family. That was only the beginning.

Chapter Fourteen
BACK TO NEBRASKA

After Jack was discharged from the hospital, we stayed in our Boston apartment for another two weeks to rule out any post-surgical issues and receive final pathological results.

When we left Boston, our medical plan was to carefully watch and wait to see if the leftover substance in Jack's head was scar tissue or tumor. Had a complete resection occurred, Jack's medical nightmare was potentially over. Only time would tell. We were due back in Boston in January of 2012. Until then, it was time to fully recover.

We returned to Nebraska on the second-to-last Saturday of October. Our Huskers were playing at Minnesota. When we got back to Atkinson, our driveway was covered in chalk and a sign greeted us from the yard. Jack's daycare provider Barb Schroeder was there with the neighbor kids, still scrawling welcome-home messages on the concrete.

Wanting to show everyone how big and tough he was, Jack went to the garage and grabbed his bike. Asking no permission, he hopped on it and charged down the driveway—without a helmet. Despite the stitches still in his head, Jack was thrilled to be home. That was our Jack…tough as nails. Determined. Loving life.

The following Saturday, Nebraska played top-ten-ranked Michigan State in Lincoln. The University of Nebraska reached out and asked us if we wanted to watch the game from a skybox. We accepted the generous invitation from Huskers booster Dick Herman.

After arriving at the stadium, we were escorted down to the sideline to watch the Huskers warm up. At one point, Rex trotted over to say hello to Jack. Rex gently placed his hand on Jack's head, and they shared a handshake. I had the opportunity to capture one of the most poignant photographs of Jack's journey. The silhouette of that photo became the logo for the Team Jack Foundation a year later.

The Huskers went on to beat Michigan State. Rex carried the ball thirty-five times for more than one-hundred-thirty yards; he even had a twenty-seven yard touchdown reception. He scored no less than three touchdowns that day.

At the conclusion of the regular season in 2011, Jack was invited to attend a Husker bowl practice (even though Head Coach Bo Pelini had previously declared practices "closed to the public.") Rex had found an exception to the rule.

On December 19th, just a little over two months after Jack's second surgery, he and Rex hung out once more. After the practice, something very special happened.

As Coach Bo called his players in, he allowed Rex the opportunity to introduce Jack to his teammates. They asked Jack to "break it down." That tiny little boy yelled, "Huskers on three! One, two…three!" The team exploded, "Huskers!"

And then, of course, Jack and Rex had to have another footrace.

As I walked off the practice field with Rex, I confided in him. What Rex had done for Jack—wearing his wristband, doing media interviews about him, and being an endless source of strength—was unlike anything anyone had ever done for our son. Quite honestly, it felt otherworldly. In that moment, I told Rex that we believed the surgery went so well due to all the prayer support he'd recruited for us.

Rex visibly took the compliment to heart. To this day, it is still the tie that binds. Rex helped save Jack's life.

Around the time of our visit to the Huskers practice, Keith Zimmer introduced me to Uplifting Athletes. This incredible non-profit organization, I learned, was formed for the sole purpose of raising research money and awareness for rare diseases. Started by Scott Shirley (a former wide receiver from Penn State), the non-profit associated with Division I football programs throughout the country. Each division could start a chapter, choose a rare disease, and then start raising money to fight that disease.

Additional programming also included an annual award called the Rare Disease Champion Award. The trophy is the silhouette of Mark Herzlich, the former Boston College player, Super Bowl champ, New York Giant—and cancer survivor. Recognizing that Rex Burkhead more than fit the criteria for the Rare Disease Champion Award, Zimmer asked me to write a nomination letter to Uplifting Athletes. I figured it was a long shot, but it was the least I could do.

Not too long after, we were thrilled to learn that Uplifting Athletes had chosen Rex Burkhead as one of four finalists. He would go up against athletes from the likes of UCLA, Penn State, and NC State. The winner would be chosen through an online voting system.

Notorious for dominating online polls, Husker fans came out in droves. Over seventy-six thousand votes were cast for Rex. In February of 2012, he received the prestigious honor of that trophy.

He was officially recognized as the award's recipient at the final Nebraska Football Spring Game of his Husker football career. On that day, the Hoffman and Burkhead families huddled beneath Memorial Stadium and covered the awarding logistics. Also present were Tom Osborne, Jan Berringer—and many grandparents, of course.

Everyone bounced with excitement. Nearly seventy-thousand Huskers fans were going to get to learn about Jack, Rex's involvement, and the dire need for pediatric brain cancer awareness and funding.

Then, suddenly, a huge thunderstorm swept over Lincoln. The Red-White Game was cancelled, as was the pregame award celebration. Despite our genuine disappointment, we got to spend nearly two hours with Rex and his family.

In reality, we had other things on our minds at that time. In less than five days, Jack would undergo a critical MRI at Boston Children's Hospital.

The weather was nothing to worry about.

The night before the rained-out game in Lincoln, we'd gone to dinner with Scott Shirley. He shared many stories over the meal. We learned how and why this twenty-something-year-old engineering student had started one of the most exciting non-profits in the country. Our conversation lit a fire in me I'd never known before. I changed. How I thought about Jack's disease also changed—in a major way.

Scott shared that during his junior year at Penn State, his father was diagnosed with kidney cancer. After helping his dad through treatment, Scott learned that his father was going to die. And the reason he was going to die was because his disease had a less than twenty percent survival rate…and research for that disease was heavily underfunded. At least, until Scott came along.

Scott recollected how he ranted to his fellow teammate and roommate, Damone Jones, one night. He was irate about the terribly limited treatment options for those with kidney cancer. Damone looked at Scott and said, "Hey, we're Penn State football. Let's do something about it."

The following spring, the Penn State team started a fundraiser called Lift for Life. Two years later, Uplifting Athletes was born, and Scott and his teammates actively helped fund clinical trials for kidney cancer research.

I relayed to Scott how distressing and archaic brain cancer treatments and chemotherapies were. I explained that the chemotherapy Jack would likely have was twenty-five-years old. He nodded knowingly, clearly having heard this conversation before.

His next words were transformative. "Andy, you can do something about it. Listen. My dad lived to within six months of a clinical trial that our football team helped fund. I nearly helped save his life."

I felt I was listening to a wizard. Could I really make that kind of a difference in my son's life? Did I need to become instrumental to his treatment from an outside avenue?

Prior to that evening, our family had never raised or donated one single dollar to cancer research. Zero. We were too self-absorbed.

Scott continued.

"But," Scott continued, "You gotta go. You have to run as fast as you can and as hard as you can. You can make a difference. Jack is still alive, and if I were you, I would do everything in my power to help fund research and clinical trials. And you can't wait. You have to do it now."

I walked away from that dinner with a single resounding message.

I have to go…Now!

Chapter Fifteen

UNEXPECTED INSPIRATION

A few days after seeing Scott, we learned that Jack would indeed require chemotherapy. He hadn't had a single seizure and was asymptomatic of tumor progression, but the tumor had grown back substantially. The spot in the nook was tumor—not scar tissue.

Jack's treatment options were limited. We were presented with two first-line chemotherapy options, both of which were markedly destructive to the body. Option number one was twenty-five-years old and could cause liver and kidney damage or permanent neuropathy. Option number two had the potential to cause a secondary cancer—leukemia.

What a kick in the shins.

As per usual, we didn't have time to feel sorry for ourselves. We had a port surgery to schedule and a chemotherapy regime to choose. God was setting the table for us, though.

I refer to cancer therapies as "scorched-earth chemo." They're like a forest fire. The tumor is one tree—but the entire national park goes down with it. Believe it or not, we give Carboplatin and Vincristine to children. They're so toxic that they physically burn skin upon contact. Infusion center nurses have to handle it with protective gloves, yet it's hooked up and pumped into kids.

Carboplatin is dumb, especially compared to the dozens of "smart" drugs that are currently being developed for adults. Smart drugs take a targeted approach. Their answer to taking down that one tree is a roaring chainsaw. Effective, right? Unless you're a child.

So, kidney failure or leukemia? We chose kidney failure and enrolled Jack in treatment in Omaha. This treatment required one trip a week for sixty weeks. The endeavor involved a full eight hours in the car and six hours of infusion for our son.

The first money we ever made for child brain cancer research was through a nonprofit called CureSearch. In June of 2012, just sixty days after Jack began chemotherapy, we organized a team for the annual cancer walk in Omaha. Jack's infusion nurses were very supportive and encouraged us to participate. We raised over eleven thousand dollars. We were even joined by Rex and a few teammates. Rex, of course, had to get special permission from the NCAA folks to attend the event.

Through an agreement with CureSearch, our funds were for the Team Jack Legacy Fund (specifically sponsored by CureSearch). This was essentially a sub-account under the CureSearch 501(c)(3), which could be self-directed by me and my wife. This was the precursor to the Team Jack Foundation.

Following the walk, we were jazzed. Our first real effort toward raising money was a huge success. Our walk team even scored third place.

We were on a roll and hungry to take on more.

A week later, I was visiting with fellow attorney Mike Flood on the phone. We were trying to settle a case and prevent it from blowing up and going to court. In addition to being a lawyer at that time, Mike was the Speaker of the House for the Nebraska Legislature. A true Nebraskan entrepreneur, Mike also owned several Nebraska radio stations, including two in Norfolk.

During our visit, Mike made the mistake of asking me about how Jack was doing. I quickly gave him a status update and then started complaining about the horrible 1980s medication Jack was taking.

Mike then told me that he knew a bit about cancer fundraising. He explained how his country radio station's "radiothon" raised over two hundred thousand dollars each year for St. Jude's Children's Research Hospital. His other station, 94 Rock, was a Husker Sports Network affiliate.

"Andy," Mike said, "when you're coming through Norfolk sometime, look me up. Let's get together and talk. I think we can figure something out to help you get where you want to go."

I told Mike that there was nothing more important and I'd be in Norfolk at his earliest convenience.

"How about Monday?" he asked.

"Done. See you then," I excitedly confirmed.

When I arrived at Mike's radio station, I was ushered into a conference room. I was immediately joined by a half-dozen broadcasters, ad salespersons, and others. I again shared Jack's story and emphasized the desperate need for funding and awareness. My audience, while captivated, immediately began firing questions at me.

"How about a t-shirt that is licensed by the University of Nebraska?" Mike suggested. "I have a meeting next week with their Athletic Director Tom Osborne, and I could talk to him about it. Tom is a great guy; I think he'd do it."

The plan unfolded. We would have red t-shirts with the official Huskers "N" printed on them. The words "Team Jack" would sit on top. The slogan, "Fighting for a victory in the battle against pediatric brain cancer," would later be added (at the suggestion of none other than Keith Zimmer). Mike thought he could reach out to all of the other Husker Sports Network affiliate stations and persuade them to promote the shirts. Each station could select a store to sell the shirts, which would also promote the stores themselves.

A bold Mike Flood then suggested that we find underwriting to cover all of the printing costs—so all profits could benefit pediatric brain cancer research.

We set a goal to sell ten thousand t-shirts.

Over the next thirty days, everyone busted ass. Mike reached out to his radio station buddies, I gathered artwork and t-shirts bids, and together we reached out to potential funders for the project.

Then reality smacked us in the face. While we were able to find a pair of small donors for the project, we did not have enough funds secured to print that many shirts. Because this would be flash promotions over a series of weekends, the t-shirts had to be printed and ordered in bulk before said promotion. We needed thirty thousand to pull this off…and we had five thousand dollars pledged.

By mid-August, the t-shirt project was on life support. Just days away from pulling the plug, I called my local banker. I gave him the sales pitch—the need for research funding, the great potential of the project, and the impact that it could have.

At the end of the conversation, he had only one question: "How much do you need?"

"I need a twenty-five-thousand-dollar unsecured line of credit," I replied. "…And I'll probably max that out right away on the first round of printing."

"Let's do it," he remarked. "I know you'll be good for it if you don't sell enough t-shirts. But I also know that won't happen. I know how it goes when you get behind something, Andy."

He knew I was lighting myself on fire.

As soon as I hung up the phone, I called Mike to tell him that we were all set. The next call was to Art F/X in Lincoln, and we hit the print button.

One nice thing about living near relatives is that they can easily be sounding boards. I'll never forget the first time I talked about "the t-shirt project" with my dad, Jack's Grandpa Gary. A seasoned businessman yet conservative farmer and rancher, this German man always had an opinion.

"I wouldn't get too carried away with this shirt deal, Andy," he warned. "That's a lot of t-shirts. I'd maybe start out with three or four hundred. No more than that."

I'd called him to borrow his twenty-foot enclosed trailer to pick up and distribute sixty-five hundred shirts (which were clearly already ordered).

Then he instantly switched from business advisor to father. "Well, let me help you. I'll go with you to Lincoln and help deliver shirts."

A few days later, he and I were headed down the highway to Lincoln. It wouldn't be the last trip, either.

My dad is a hero.

Chapter Sixteen

LIGHT YOURSELF ON FIRE

I was so excited about the t-shirts. And then…

Holy boxes. Six thousand five hundred t-shirts entirely fills a twenty-foot enclosed trailer.

After getting the shirts, we headed to Omaha to make the first delivery at Husker Hounds. From there, it was back to Lincoln to drop off at Husker Headquarters…then to Grand Island, Albion, Columbus, O'Neill, and Atkinson. With each delivery, we snapped a picture of the store owner holding up a shirt. All photos were posted for our thirty-five hundred Facebook followers. Likes and comments piled up.

Two days later, I traveled back to Lincoln for the first Huskers home game. I would sell shirts at the HuskerMax tailgate party, thanks to our buddy David Max. (What a kind soul.) On that sweltering Saturday in August, we sold about fifty shirts. I was terrified.

On top of that, our golden boy Rex suffered a potentially season-ending injury that same day. If Rex went down, I knew our t-shirt extravaganza was over. Everyone associated Rex with Team Jack. I went from terrified to completely sickened.

But the silver lining on that sticky, sweaty Saturday was meeting Monica Waggoner. As I sat there peddling shirts like a carnival worker, a lady and her sister walked up to our booth—already wearing Team Jack t-shirts. She stepped up to me with a tear in her eye and asked, "Can I give you a hug?"

After introducing herself, Monica then proceeded to tell me that she'd lost her son Nathan to brain cancer in 2010. Needless to say, she was thrilled that we were raising money and awareness for the disease. She immediately became a family friend. She was also the first Nebraska "brain cancer parent" I had ever met. Our team had a new teammate, and she was a great one.

One thousand…six hundred…and sixty-seven was the magic "get out of debt" number. If I didn't sell at least that many shirts, the grand project would be a grand failure. My wife, while supportive, was on edge. Having already spent substantial personal wealth battling Jack's brain tumor in Boston, we weren't necessarily in the best position to absorb a twenty-five thousand dollar hit.

Throughout that first weekend, with store allocations and game-day sales, we sold maybe two hundred fifty t-shirts—max. I was freaking out, but Mike Flood and crew at 94 Rock had a very calming effect.

"Wait for radio," Mike advised me on the following Monday. "Once the radio stations start promoting this, it's going to take off like you wouldn't believe."

His words were prophetic.

The goal was to have a Team Jack gathering for the Nebraska-Wisconsin game in about three weeks.

As radio stations in Norfolk, Grand Island, Kearney, Lincoln, Sidney, North Platte, Broken Bow, Chadron, Scottsbluff, Hastings, O'Neill, Omaha, and other places got rolling with their promotions, our little project took on a life of its own. By the end of September, nearly twenty thousand t-shirts had been printed and nearly fifteen thousand had sold.

T-shirts continued flying off the shelves well past the Nebraska-Wisconsin game. People genuinely liked the shirts and supporting pediatric brain cancer research. Nebraska's statewide media support was unbelievable.

Our project spawned a series of other fundraisers for months to come. A movement was afoot, and its effects were vast. Volunteer organizations and Nebraska businesses started taking note.

Suddenly, we were receiving donations in addition to our t-shirt profits.

In the wings, Keith Zimmer had not forgotten about Rex's missed award ceremony. Keith suggested that Nebraska host a brain cancer awareness game each fall—and at the first one, Jack and another survivor should lead the Huskers in a tunnel walk.

It turned out that our Jack and Isaiah Casillas were two lucky little boys. Those guys walked with the Huskers from the locker room to the entrance of Memorial Stadium. And this was the same game that nearly twenty thousand Huskers fans wore shirts reading "Team Jack."

Heartbreakingly, Isaiah died on December 2nd, 2012…just sixty-five days after he bravely led the Huskers through the tunnel.

Isaiah's father, Patrick, remained involved with our foundation. He had unbelievable strength and courage through his son's journey, and his optimism was steadfast.

Before Jack was diagnosed, I had never met another child with a brain tumor. I also had never been to a child's funeral. When Isaiah died, it was difficult to tell Jack. Our son didn't go to the funeral; he was on chemotherapy and had just turned seven.

My father made the four-hour trek with me to Ogallala for Isaiah's funeral. My chest aches every time I remember the cloud of balloons they released into the sky in his memory. While the Huskers didn't score a touchdown that day, heaven sure did.

Unbeknownst to essentially everyone except my wife, I had sent a private letter to a prominent Nebraskan shortly after spending time with Scott Shirley. The letter was to Sid Dinsdale, the President of Pinnacle Bancorp, Inc.—a large Nebraska-based banking business. (Two years later, the Huskers' new basketball arena would be named Pinnacle Bank Arena.) My letter outlined my deep disappointment in the lack of brain cancer research funding and the massive need for aid. I wrote the letter to him as a father. I had never met Sid.

In early September of 2012, I received a phone call from Randy Hupp at the local Pinnacle Bank in O'Neill. He asked that I come over and visit with him, per the request of Mr. Dinsdale.

I rushed there immediately.

Soon after my arrival, Mr. Hupp told me some amazing news.

Mr. Dinsdale and Pinnacle Bank, based on one letter, were going to donate a hundred thousand dollars to pediatric brain cancer research in honor of Jack. There was only one stipulation: the gift needed to be confidential. They did not want a pat on the back. It was personal. They wanted to do it for Jack—and all the children like him. I cried.

The Dinsdale family, due to our insistent urging, graciously allowed us to publicize their gift. We wanted it to inspire others. A year later, a choked-up Sid Dinsdale received the first-ever Team Jack Foundation Teammate of the Year Award in Atkinson. I will never forget his stirring acceptance speech or his generosity.

Since our first t-shirt printing, we'd raised over three hundred thousand dollars. One crazy, pissed-off dad and his family had lit themselves on fire, and our home state had come to the rescue.

On January 17th, 2013 (the anniversary of the death of Don Shirley, Scott's father), our family presented Dana-Farber Cancer Institute with a check for two hundred seventy-five thousand dollars for child brain cancer research. What we had left over in the account would be used for our next project.

Having been such a huge part of the t-shirt project, Grandpa Gary and Grandma Karen came to Boston with us to present the check.

On the trip home, I was full of electricity. About midway, I began talking about doing another t-shirt project. Thirty days later, I asked the University of Nebraska to approve another shirt. This one would be for May—brain tumor awareness month. It would don the Huskers Iron "N" and a gray ribbon woven through the word "Believe." By March 1st, 2013, the second shirt was approved.

Shortly after January 1st, 2013, my wife and I had decided to form the Team Jack Foundation. We formed our own 501(c)(3) and then created our website. It was basic but perfect.

By April 1st, 2013, our foundation was in full swing. We had raised nearly thirty thousand dollars more for research and were excited about the direction we were heading.

As Rex Burkhead was done with college football, he was newly available to help with fundraising events. Unfortunately, we were far from fundraising experts at that time. Despite the success from the previous t-shirt project, we were in uncharted territory—trying to raise money with a fledgling foundation.

Chapter Seventeen

THE RUN

On Wednesday, April 3rd, Jack had an MRI at Boston Children's Hospital. It revealed that the tumor was still responding to treatment. In fact, it was shrinking.

On the following Friday, we'd just put the kids down and were settling in for our nightly visit. My phone rang at 9:30 p.m. It was an unknown number. I flashed my phone at Bri.

"Do you know this number?" I asked.

"I wouldn't answer it," she said.

Right before the phone stopped ringing, I decided to answer it.

"This is Andy," I said.

"Hey, Andy. This is Coach Jeff Jamrog with the University of Nebraska at Lincoln. How are you doing?"

"Hi, Coach; how you doing?" I responded.

"Andy, Coach Bo, myself, and some of the other coaches came up with kind of a crazy idea tonight. We were wondering—is Jack coming to the Spring Game tomorrow?"

"Yeah, Coach, we are planning on coming down tomorrow…" I answered. "What's going on?"

"Well, we were wondering what you would think about Jack suiting up and scoring a touchdown. We thought it would be awesome if he could come in for the last play of the game, maybe take a hand off from the five-yard line. We thought this would really be something great for Jack. A sort of Make-A-Wish experience."

Sensing my hesitation, he shared an additional thought: "Did you see the Cal spring game earlier this year when Marshawn Lynch came back from the NFL and scored a touchdown? It was kinda cool."

I had no clue what he was talking about, but he convinced me.

I hung up the phone and turned to my frowning wife. She was not exactly a fan.

"Andy, that is a lot to ask of a seven-year-old boy. I'm not sure he should do it." She exhaled. "Besides, he's already had so much attention on him…I just don't think he needs this kind of spotlight."

Bri, my small-town introvert, was understandably concerned. But by 10 p.m., I had talked her into it. I called Coach Jamrog back and told him that Jack was in.

One detail wasn't pinned down. Coach Jamrog and I were unsure what the heck Jack would wear for his on-field performance. When Jack was three years old, he'd received a Franklin uniform from Walmart for his birthday. It had a chintzy number 7 jersey, pants that no longer fit, skimpy shoulder pads, and an oversized plastic helmet with a red "N." We snagged the helmet and shoulder pads.

Our family is exceedingly proud of our Huskers football allegiance. My older brother had been a 1993 Huskers walk-on. With three National Championships and three Conference Championship rings in his favor, Mike played twenty-nine snaps over four years as a nose guard. An eight-man football player, he was a standout scout teamer for Tommie Frazier and company during his Huskers tenure.

While Mike played at Nebraska, he was continuously bringing home Huskers swag. Adidas shoes, coats, shirts, duffel bags—you name it, he had it. At one point, he even brought home a pair of his Huskers practice pants, shining white with a red stripe. As a high schooler, I wore them to my own practices. I was the only one on the team with official Huskers practice pants. Eventually, Mom gave them a final wash and put them with the rest of my junk. For fifteen years, those pants rested in the basement of wherever I lived. They probably should have been thrown out.

After hanging up with Coach Jamrog, I went digging. After about five minutes, I uncovered the pants—shriveled up, but functional. I also found a purple Spencer-Naper Pirate football belt. I added these items to the uniform.

The uniform's final touch was simple: my son would wear his Rex Burkhead autographed jersey.

After getting shaved and showered the next morning, I trudged into Jack's room, proud and excited to share the exciting news. It was 6 a.m. Jack was tired. He was so tired, in fact, that his initial reaction was not favorable. Jack generally needed lots of sleep to avoid crabbiness. And on this morning, he was definitely crabby.

After rousing him from bed, I ushered him downstairs to try on his football uniform, which was laid out on the kitchen table. He quickly put it on and posed for a picture. I immediately texted the picture to Coach Jamrog, seeking his approval.

Coach responded, "Looks great. That'll be awesome."

I was grateful to avoid shopping in Lincoln on a Saturday morning.

While excited about what lay ahead, there was a voice of caution in Jack's head. Like his mother, he was hesitant about having so much attention drawn to him.

By 6:30 a.m., we were locked and loaded. Jack, Ava, myself, and our family friend Chris and his son Drake headed down the road. This crew had made the trip before. Same drill. Get in the car, hold your potty, and we'll be there in four hours. Chris and I both subscribed to hurrying up and just getting there…I liked traveling with him.

Just outside of St. Edward, my phone rang. It was Bri.

"You know, Andy, I've been thinking," she started. "If Jack doesn't want to run the ball at the game, make sure you tell him he doesn't have to. Make sure you tell him that if he is scared, if he doesn't want to do it, that it's okay. Promise me you'll give him that option."

In a halfhearted tone, which she could easily detect, I promised her I would give him that choice. As I spoke, Chris shot me an unforgettable smirk. He and I both knew what was going to happen. We'd both played football and were huge Huskers fans. Jack would score a touchdown on that day, come hell or high water.

Upon arriving in Lincoln, we immediately went up to the coaches' offices. Coaches and players alike slipped by, shook my hand, and gave the kids high-fives. We "went over the program" with Coach Jamrog.

Around 11:00 a.m., the players gathered in the team meeting room. That would be a big day for the Huskers. Every Nebraska Football Spring Game usually had about sixty thousand attending fans.

We hung out on the side of the meeting for a while…and then Coach Bo started talking.

"You guys all know Jack," he began, motioning for Jack and me to stand beside him. "This is the toughest kid in Nebraska. We all know that. Well, today, he is going to play with all of you. At some point in the fourth quarter, Jack's gonna come onto the field and score a touchdown. Today, he's a Cornhusker."

The room exploded.

Coach Bo couldn't help but join in their enthusiasm. The quick-witted coach yelled toward defensive linebacker Zaire Anderson, "Zaire, don't tackle him!" Laughter resounded.

We received our instructions to go and sit up in Coach Bo's family suite in the East Stadium and have a fantastic time. We would later be guided down to the sidelines by Chris Anderson, a longtime Athletic Department assistant.

Jack had been in chemotherapy for eleven months by that time. He was a bit frail and had signs of neuropathy in his ankles due to his taking Vincristine. His physical condition aside, his biggest concern was understanding how to react in a real game. Up to that point in time, Jack had never played a single down of organized football. He'd only tossed the football with his old man in our backyard.

Admittedly, Jack knew what the option was, what the chair route was, and also routes such as flag, post, or curl. He could do a nice five-and-out or ten-and-in, too. He'd already known that Zac Taylor was the Huskers starting quarterback when he was only three years old. He had grown up watching all levels of football.

Anyone who has ever stepped onto the field at Memorial Stadium can tell you about the immediate rush of euphoric adrenaline. I felt it for the first time when I was in fifth grade. And that was when the stadium was completely empty.

Although Jack was clearly no stranger to the turf of that field, this event would be completely different than racing around with Rex.

"Jack, do you see that white line, right there?" I asked my son during the first half, pointing to the sideline.

"That one right there, Dad?" he asked, pointing his tiny finger.

"No, Jack. The white line that runs north to south." I motioned left to right from the booth.

"Okay, yeah…the one with the players standing by it," he replied.

"Yes, that line."

"What about that line, Dad?"

"That's the out-of-bounds line. Whatever you do, do not cross that line. If you run out-of-bounds, the play is over," I explained.

"Okay, Dad. I understand. Do not run out-of-bounds." He nodded in confirmation.

A few plays later, I pointed out the touchdown line. From the top deck of Memorial Stadium, there are piles of white lines. Especially to the eyes of a little boy.

"Jack, you know when a touchdown is scored, right?" I inquired.

"Yeah, Dad. It's when they run towards the goal post," he remarked.

"That's right, Jack; but when they cross that last white line, that's when it's a touchdown."

I knew he understood what a touchdown was, but I thought a gentle reminder might calm his anxiety. However, the conversation actually made me more nervous.

What if Jack stops at the five-yard line? I worried.

Sensing my concern, Jack asked, "Dad, how will I know when I scored a touchdown?"

I thought for a moment. Then it hit me.

"Jack, just run until you hit the fence."

He gave me a courageous smile and agreed to the plan.

At halftime, we headed clear to the north end of the sixth floor. In that empty hallway, we went over the play possibilities. We again practiced Jack's stance. Then we practiced hand-offs, toss sweeps, and option pitches. Left, right, and up-the-gut. That was probably the most poignant father-son football practice in the history of Memorial Stadium. I would never forget it, at least.

With about ten minutes left in the third quarter, my cell phone rang. It was one of the team's graduate assistants.

"Hey, Andy, why don't you and Jack go ahead and come on down. There's been a change in plans…I think we're going to move Jack's play up so it's not right at the end."

With that, we all grabbed our stuff and took the elevator downstairs. Jack gripped the strap of his backpack that held his secret football uniform.

Once we made it to the sideline, Jack and I were absorbed into the team and coaches. Jack, still in street clothes, was prompted to get changed.

"You want me to change right here?!" he proclaimed.

"Yes, Jack. We'll do it real quick. No one will notice," I promised. "These guys will shield you so no one will see you in your underwear."

Instantly, half-dozen offensive linemen huddled around me and my son. Those Huskers physically kept secret that a seven-year-old had bared his tighty-whities on the Memorial Stadium sideline. Soon after, the huddling players fell away to display four-foot-something Jack decked out in Huskers regalia. My son was the Huskers Clark Kent.

Initially, the situation felt a little odd. Not just for Jack, but for his father, too. Some of the players seemed a little funny about the whole thing. However, with his good buddy C.J. Zimmerer standing beside him in full pads, Jack was easily comforted. Then we had the pleasure of Rex joining us. He and his family were in town for the game.

As the clock wound down, the coaches started looking over to us.

"How close do we need to get it for Jack?" I overheard Bo Pelini ask Coach Jamrog.

Coach Jamrog quickly made his way over to me. "How far do you think Jack could run?" he asked.

I thought for a split second—and then the proud father inside could not resist. I blurted out, "He could race Rex Burkhead a full hundred yards, so wherever you want to run the play will work!"

The coaches went back to work, jockeying the field position just right. Meanwhile, Jack was summoned over to the bench, where former Huskers starting quarterback and graduate assistant Joe Ganz drew up a play on a whiteboard. Taylor Martinez and C.J. Zimmerer watched, as well. Coach Ganz sketched a simple stretch zone play: Jack would get the ball, run right, turn toward the end zone, and run for the touchdown.

As I watched Ganz explain the play, I could see in Jack's face and body language that not everything was sinking in. This was markedly different than anything he had ever done in his life.

I chimed in. "Jack, Taylor is going to hand you the ball, and then you are going to run right—that way, okay, Jack?" I physically motioned what the play read.

Despite any doubts I had, I kept repeating the basics. No out-of-bounds, no fumbles, score the touchdown. Little did I know, he absorbed and hung onto every word I spoke. He trusted his dad and would follow his advice.

As soon as the breakout session with Coach Ganz ended, I grabbed Taylor. I told him to be prepared for Jack to potentially go the wrong way.

Suddenly, the whistle blew, and Jack was called to join the team and Coach Bo on the field near the sideline. I hustled over there with him.

My mind raced frantically. I can't imagine what was going through my son's head.

Then Jack jaunted out onto the field. This was it—and my thoughts swirled. I could've puked right before the play started.

The public announcer said Jack's name, and the crowd began cheering. Taylor was in the shotgun stance, getting ready to take the hike.

"Set, hut!" Taylor yelled as he clapped his hands. He swiftly received the snap and handed the ball off to Jack, who stood to his left.

Initially, Jack took off to the left.

As the entire line began zone-blocking to the right, Taylor quickly redirected Jack to follow his blockers on his right. The hole in the line opened up as my son bolted east-west. As he headed toward the sideline, I was in awe behind my camera. I could not believe what I was observing. He was running right at me.

Then, Jack curved to face the end zone. I couldn't help myself and walked ten yards out onto the field to watch him travel. Moments later, the entire bench cleared in front of me and Jack vanished from my sight. I couldn't see him run the last forty yards.

A lightning bolt of fear traveled my spine when I lost my view of Jack…but my fears completely evaporated as the stadium rumbled into a thunderous wave of cheers.

I always thought it cliché to describe something as the "biggest" or "loudest" or "best" or whatever. But to me, the sound was heavenly.

And Taylor Martinez, one of the Huskers' all-time offensive leaders, confirmed it in the days following the game. "That was the loudest I have ever heard that stadium," Taylor recalled. "It was the loudest roar…It was amazing. It was something I will never forget."

And to be honest, of all the Huskers games I'd seen, I had to agree with him. And it was all for my son.

The memory of that day joyously bewilders me. It still hasn't sunk in.

I hope it never does.

Meanwhile, Jack's mom sat in our living room back in Atkinson. She'd been nervously watching the game unfold on the TV.

 "I was just so anxious when he took the field," Bri said. "All I cared was that he didn't fall down or fumble the ball. I was nauseous."

It would be several hours after Jack's run before I could connect with Bri.

Immediately after his run, Jack hit the sideline—entirely unaware of what he'd just accomplished. He knew he'd scored a touchdown; he knew it'd been a blast. But he didn't know that he'd just been introduced to all of America. Nor did I.

All of the coaches congratulated Jack. Some of my favorite photos from the run depict Coach Bo patting Jack on the back with a huge grin. Players threw him high-fives.

Once things calmed on the sideline, Rex came over to hang out with us. He gave me a huge hug. We both blinked away tears. Rex was ecstatic for Jack.

Robyn and Rick Burkhead—the parents of an angel—are amazing people. They also found us on the sideline and covered us with love and hugs. Rick smiled as if his own son had scored the touchdown. Robyn cried, repeatedly patting Jack on the back, telling him how proud she was.

 After a few more minutes, Jack and I were ushered toward a swarming group of cameras and reporters roped along the sideline. I had never been to an impromptu postgame press conference—and, obviously, neither had Jack.

There were around twenty reporters gathered, all leaning in to chat. I had no clue that the videos and quotes captured would appear a few hours later on ESPN *SportsCenter*, The Associated Press, and *USA Today*. (And then in daily papers across the United States.)

In the middle of being interviewed, an assistant coach grabbed us. "Coach Bo needs you guys in the locker room; follow me," he said.

Jack and I hustled off of the field, through the tunnel, and into the locker room. When we arrived, Coach Bo was addressing a huddled team for postgame comments.

"All right, everybody, let's hear it for Jack—our player of the game!" Coach Bo called out.

I could see that Coach Bo was holding the game ball and was about to do the unthinkable—present it to Jack. I worked my way through the boys, camera at the ready, and listened to Bo's next words.

"Jack, you had an amazing run today," Coach said, looking down at my son. "This is your game ball. One more time! Let's hear it for Jack!"

The room vibrated with sound.

And then, Coach Bo said, "Let's take a knee."

It was the ceremonial postgame moment of silence, a time for reflection and prayer.

I glanced over and saw Coach Bo holding Jack's hand.

That's the Coach Bo we know. That's the real Coach Bo—putting others before himself.

After the game, Jack, Chris, Drake, Ava, and I headed to a bar and grill to have supper with the Burkhead family. We planned to catch some of the Final Four and recap the day together. The kids played pool as the adults relaxed. We were oblivious to what was happening in the outside world. The warmth of the company and the game's memories held us tightly.

The ride home was wild. Jack had clocked out from his workday on the football field, and all three kids played video games in the back seat of the Suburban. We wouldn't get home until around midnight, but they didn't care whatsoever.

Around 10 p.m., as we pulled through Albion, Chris flashed me his phone to show me a text from his wife, Lindsey: "Jack's play was just shown on ESPN *SportsCenter*. They had a telestrator on him."

Chris and I just looked at each other. Jack's run was going to cause more of a ripple than we'd originally thought. We started discussing possibilities for the Team Jack Foundation and what this could do for awareness. About an hour later, Lindsey texted again: "Holy Cow…Jack's run is up for *SportsCenter*'s Top 10 Plays of the Day."

By the time we got home, the kids were asleep. After carrying them to bed, I rushed to the TV. I had to see it for myself. I stayed up until 4 a.m. watching each round of *SportsCenter*. I saw the run. And I saw the crowd's reaction from a wider lens. It was amazing.

Even more amazing was that even though the NCAA basketball tournament was happening, the midnight *SportsCenter* anchor started the broadcast with, "Today was a big day in sports. It was the first day of the Final Four in NCAA Men's Basketball—but before that, we are going to take you out to Lincoln, Nebraska, where a little boy and the Nebraska Cornhuskers are our top story of the night."

After two-plus minutes of highlights and quotes, the story then detailed the growth of our movement and how Team Jack had raised over three hundred thousand dollars for child brain cancer research. *Thank you, ESPN*, I thought.

My wife kept me grounded. Around 1 a.m., she headed to bed and encouraged me to follow. I was too engulfed to follow. Eventually, as I realized I'd been watching the same stories over and over, I landed in bed, my head still spinning.

The next morning, Bri made one thing abundantly clear: "I don't care how many posts there are on Facebook, and I don't care how many news stories there are going to be about Jack and the run this morning. We are all going to church."

So we did. And I didn't even take my cell phone with me. Wasn't worth the risk.

When we got home after church, countless messages on our home phone and piles of emails greeted us. From *Good Morning America* to the NFL Network, our story was in high demand.

Before returning any phone calls, my wife and I had a very serious discussion. She posed a very pertinent question: "Is all of this media attention in Jack's best interest?"

Not an easy question to answer.

In the end, Bri and I decided that we would avail ourselves to the media—but we would do so to draw attention to the leading cause of childhood cancer deaths: brain cancer. We wanted America to know that children were dying of brain tumors due to terrible underfunding and lack of attention.

First up was ESPN…in two days.

Chapter Eighteen

THE MEDIA TOUR BEGINS

ESPN wanted to travel to Atkinson and hold an in-home interview with Jack. They traveled through a spring blizzard to reach our house.

They tore our living room apart with lights and cameras. Jack was interviewed. Bri was interviewed. I was interviewed. Between sessions, we took Chris Connelly down to our basement so he could see firsthand what Team Jack was all about.

He saw our mini fulfillment center: stacks of t-shirts, piles of wristbands, and other gear. It was the most-frequented place in the house—the "Shipping Center." Throughout the day, we told the ESPN crew about child brain cancer and the need for funding. They got sick of hearing about it. They could see, up close and personal, merely by the state of our basement alone, that our lives were entirely committed to fighting this disease.

On the following Friday night, ESPN *SportsCenter* ran the seven-minute feature. Toward the end of his interview, Jack described his field run as "super-duper awesome." Within minutes, #superduperawesome was trending on Twitter. When the story concluded, the two anchors looked at each other, hoping the other would quell pressing tears. One of them echoed, "Super. Duper. Awesome."

We watched this from the comfort of our living room that had since been put back together after ESPN left. As our children slept, Bri and I stared through the television.

The next day, ESPN ran Jack's feature every hour for nearly twelve hours straight. And each time the story was introduced, the *SportsCenter* newscasters pointed to the Team Jack bands on their wrists and described the need for funding in child brain cancer research. It just kept coming.

That afternoon, we had a group of high school volunteers come over to help fill t-shirt orders. We got six hundred out that day. By that night, we had another two thousand shirt and wristband orders. Our foundation was beyond blessed when it came to advertising.

ABC World News Tonight, CNN Headline News, CNN Morning Express, and many more came calling. By Friday of that first media week, we were exhausted; Jack and I had made over twelve national media appearances on radio and TV. There were dozens of other local media requests as well.

By the end of the week, I was also pissed. As the days had worn on, the media had grown more and more interested in the and-how-did-this-make-you-feel-as-a-father? storyline. Flavor of the week, emotional baiting.

I hated it. Self-promotion and self-gratification were in no way our goals. I grew up scooping hog shit, fixing fences on our ranch—far too busy for whatever the news spewed. I decided to fight back to keep our story focused on the right topic.

Through a Huskers friend, I was able to track down former Huskers football quarterback Zac Lee. Zac's sister was a reporter for Fox News in New York.

I called Zac and leveled with him.

"Hi, Zac…This is Jack's dad."

"Awesome story on ESPN," he immediately responded.

He clearly needed no further context as to who I was.

"You know, the only reason we opened ourselves to the media was to tell them about the need for child brain cancer research funding," I said. "But that doesn't seem to be the focus of our stories." I braced myself before asking the favor. "Do you think you could ask your sister Jenna if Fox would have any interest in our talking about child brain cancer research funding?"

"I'll give her a call," he replied.

The next day, I had a voicemail from Jenna Lee. A few days later, Jenna, the host of *Happening Now* on Fox News at that time, ran a feature story about the appalling lack of funding in child brain cancer research.

The media appearances directly tied to "The Run" stayed active throughout most of May of 2013. When the ESPN crew had been interviewing Bri upstairs, I had received a phone call from a gentleman named Mike Schnoor. He called from Norfolk to tell me that Upper Deck sports cards was interested in doing what he called a "Rookie Card."

Even though I felt too distracted for the call at the time, I listened to him explain that he had been speaking with someone named Chris Carlin from Upper Deck in California—and they wanted to create a Star Rookie Card for Jack. I thought the idea was a bit crazy, but I agreed to forward him a picture that I'd taken on the day of the run.

A few weeks later, Upper Deck issued a card for public auction with profits going to our foundation. The card itself measured approximately twelve-by-thirty inches, and it looked like a mid-sized placard. Ultimately, the foundation sold three of these cards, raising nearly thirty thousand dollars in total.

In mid-May of 2013, the card was delivered to a studio in Minneapolis, Minnesota, where James Denton, Jack, and I appeared on *Happening Now* with Jenna.

Even though we were road-weary, the table God had set for us overflowed.

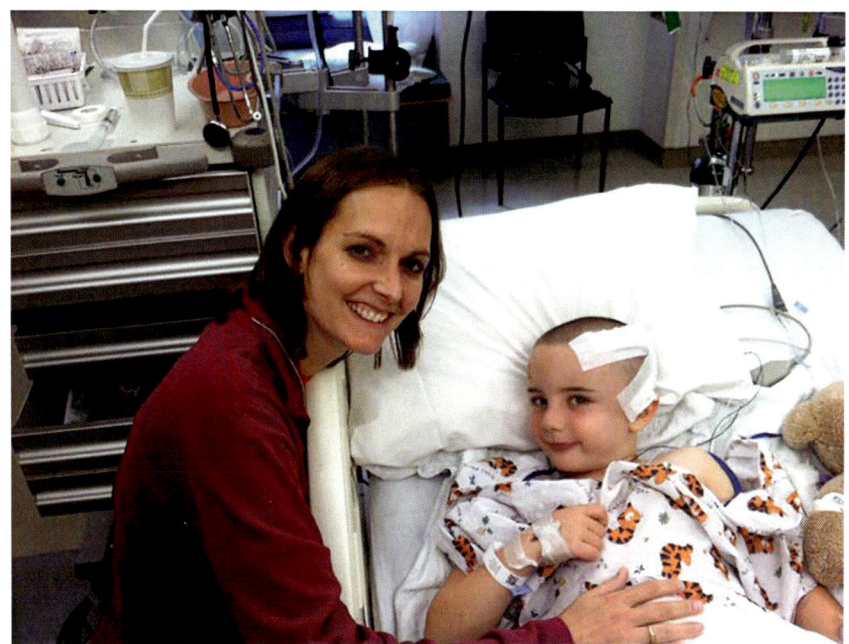

Jack and his mom, Bri, after Jack's second brain tumor surgery in Boston.

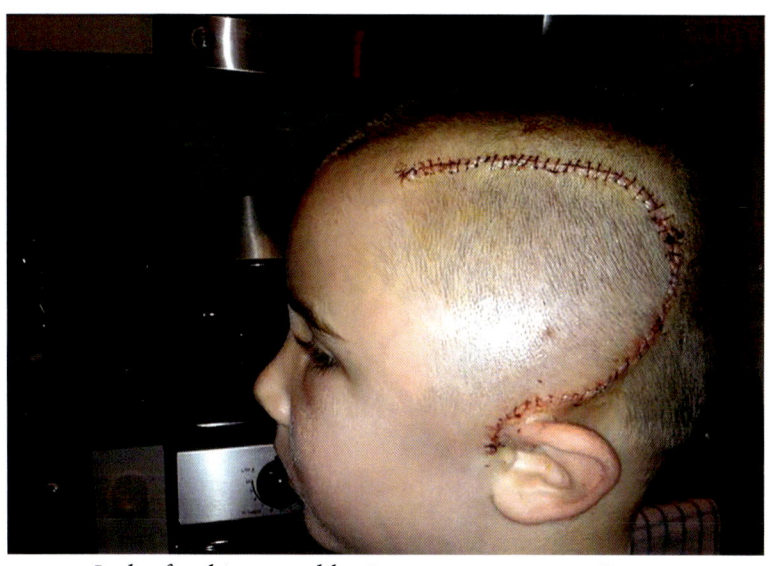

Jack after his second brain tumor surgery in Boston.

A 5-year-old boy and his favorite University of Nebraska running back, Rex Burkhead, spent a day together in 2011—eating lunch, touring the football facilities, and racing on the field. As a kid growing up in Nebraska, Jack looked up to Rex as his role model on the football field, and now, nearly a decade later, their friendship remains.

Rex signing Jack's #22 Husker "Burkhead" jersey, given to him by his parents just months earlier.

*During their first meeting, Jack asks his new friend, Rex,
if he wants to race, so they did, and Jack won.*

*At just seven years old, Jack suited up for the 2013 Nebraska
Football Spring Game. His 69-yard touchdown was watched
nationwide, helping raise awareness for pediatric brain
cancer, with which he had been diagnosed two years earlier.*

Jack and Rex at the 2013 Nebraska
Football Spring Game prior to "The Run."

Jack, then seven years old,
won the award for "Best
Moment" in Sports at the
2013 ESPY Awards.
He earned the award with
his 69-yard touchdown
run in the 2013 Nebraska
Football Spring Game.

Jack and Taylor Martinez during the 2013 Nebraska Football Spring Game. Then quarterback for the Huskers, Martinez, took the snap and handed the ball to Jack, assisting him in his 69-yard touchdown run.

Coach Bo Pelini giving Jack the game ball after his famous 69-yard touchdown during the 2013 Nebraska Football Spring Game.

*The Team Jack Family was created by the Team Jack Foundation
to bring families affected by brain cancer together for support
and to advocate for the disease. Each year, these families are
recognized at a Husker football game in September which
is dedicated to childhood brain cancer awareness.*

*Jack and Rex at a preseason
game in Kansas City after Rex
was selected by the Bengals
in the 2013 NFL draft.*

*Jack, Ava, and Reese with Rex
in October, 2015 in Cincinnati
during the Bengals vs. Chiefs
regular season game.*

Andy and Jack at Super Bowl LIII on February 3, 2019, where Rex grabbed his first Super Bowl Championship after defeating the LA Rams 13-3.

Jack and David Ortiz, also known as "Big Papi," first baseman for the Boston Red Sox, in 2013. David was excited about meeting Jack. That year the Red Sox won the World Series and Ortiz was named World Series MVP.

In September 2016, the 6th annual Betty Jane France Humanitarian Award presented by Nationwide was awarded to Andy Hoffman. With this award, the Team Jack Foundation received a $100,000 donation from The NASCAR Foundation. The award is given to a NASCAR fan who has made a profound impact on children in their local community in which Andy has done through his work at the Team Jack Foundation.

Andy with Jimmie Johnson, a seven-time NASCAR Cup Series champion, in Las Vegas at the NASCAR Cup Series Awards in December 2016.

Jack and Martin Truex, Jr., during The NASCAR Foundation's Annual Gala event in New York where Andy was awarded the Betty Jane France Humanitarian Award in November of 2016. Martin continues to be a Team Jack supporter to this day.

Andy with Eddie Vedder, Pearl Jam's front man and Andy's favorite band, at the NASCAR Cup Awards. In this photo, Andy was sharing Team Jack's mission with Vedder.

In 2012, Andy and Bri set a very simple goal: they wanted to try and raise $100,000 for childhood brain cancer research through the sale of a t-shirt. The shirt was a Team Jack shirt approved by the University of Nebraska and designed with the Husker "Iron N" logo on it. By the end of the 2012, they had sold nearly 30,000 t-shirts.

Jack and Rex at the Husker football game against Michigan State in October of 2011. This was Jack's first Husker game following his second brain tumor surgery in Boston. This photo is also the inspiration behind the Team Jack Foundation logo.

Jack and Rex at the 2012 Husker vs. Wisconsin game. This game was dedicated to childhood brain cancer awareness. During the game, Jack and Isaiah Casillas, who passed away in 2012, led the team out of the tunnel.

In April 2013, post-"The Run", President Obama invited the Hoffman Family to Washington, D.C. He spent about 15 minutes with Jack and the family along with Rex, in the Oval Office. After the meeting, President Obama gave Jack an autographed football which included the Presidential Seal.

Photos courtesy of The White House.

119

The Hoffman Family at a regular season Patriots' game at Foxboro in the fall of 2018.

Jack and Rex in Boston in front of the Ted Williams statue at Fenway Park. Ted Williams was not only one of the greatest hitters in baseball history, but he also cared deeply for children. Andy always felt a connection between this statue and the photo of Jack and Rex that later became the Team Jack logo.

Andy has been an avid runner since 2014. His marathons have included Boston (April 2014), Los Angeles (March 2015), Chicago (October 2015), and Minneapolis (2016 and 2017). Andy completed his sixth full marathon in Los Angeles in March 2020.

In April 2014, Andy ran his first full marathon, the Boston Marathon, as a charity runner for Boston Children's Hospital. During his 26.2-mile run, he dedicated each mile to a child who had been affected by brain cancer while also raising awareness for Team Jack.

Andy and Jack with Dick Vitale, Tom Crean, Nick Saban, and Mike Brey, at Dick Vitale's Gala in Sarasota, Florida, in May 2014.

In September 2019, Jack played his very first junior high football game for the West Holt Huskies. He was named ABC's "Person of the Week" as a result.

Andy, Jack, and Bri after a junior high football game in 2019.

In November 2019, Midland University Head Football Coach, Jeff Jamrog, presented Jack with a four-year, full-tuition scholarship to Midland University. In 2013, Jamrog served as the assistant coach with former Coach Bo Pelini and was a part of the planning for Jack's Spring Game touchdown.

Jack and Andy at the 2014 Team Jack
Foundation Radiothon in Lincoln, Nebraska.

Andy and Bri at Jack's first high school football game on
August 28, 2020, in their hometown of Atkinson, Nebraska.

*Andy with his siblings, Mike, Tony, and Julia, the
week of his diagnosis in Rochester, Minnesota.*

*Andy with Bri, Jack, Ava, and Reese, as well as his parents, Gary
and Karen, the day before his surgery in Rochester, Minnesota.*

*Rex showing off his custom designed Team Jack cleats
for the NFL "My Cause My Cleats" campaign.*

Rex and Jack at the 2017 Team Jack Trifecta held annually in Plano, Texas.

In January 2013, the Hoffman Family presented Dr. Mark Kieran, Dr. Liliana Goumnerova, and Dr. Nicole Ulrich at the Dana-Farber Cancer Institute with a $275,000 check for child brain cancer research.

In 2015, the Team Jack Foundation presented the University of Nebraska Medical Center (Ken Cowan, MD, PhD, Director of the Fred and Pamela Buffett Cancer Center) a check for a $1.5 million commitment, matched by the State of Nebraska, to create a $3 million pediatric brain tumor program in Nebraska. As of February 2018, the Team Jack Foundation has committed $6.5 million to the University for this program.

In September 2019, the Hoffman Family traveled to Boston for a checkup for Jack. During their visit, they were able to see Rex play in the Patriots vs. Steelers season opener.

*In Fall of 2019, Andy and Jack were honored by the invitation to be on **College GameDay** in Lincoln, Nebraska. Andy used the invite to educate people about brain cancer in kids.*

Jack, with his cousin and best buddy, Hudson Hoffman, and Rex, after the AFC championship in Kansas City. This photo was taken after Jack suffered from a nearly half-hour seizure. Jack was able to go back to the game just in time to see Rex score back-to-back touchdowns to punch the Patriots' ticket to Super Bowl LIII.

The Hoffmans at the childhood brain cancer awareness game at Memorial Stadium in Lincoln, Nebraska, in 2016.

Andy, Bri, and Jack with Larry the Cable Guy and Jeff Foxworthy at a Team Jack fundraiser in Spring of 2014. Larry the Cable Guy has been a strong supporter of Team Jack since the beginning.

Jack and the late Stuart Scott at the 2013 ESPY Awards.

Chapter Nineteen

THE PRESIDENT WILL
SEE YOU NOW

It was difficult sorting through life in the days that followed Jack's touchdown run. Even a German magazine wanted to publish an article and needed photos. The NFL Network needed a radio interview. Cards and letters came in from all over the country. People were amazing. Perhaps one of the most interesting letters was from the man who played Yoda in the first three Star Wars films. He even sent Jack gifts.

Newspaper clippings about Jack's run arrived constantly. He even received handmade wooden gifts.

As I reflect back on that time, I am still overwhelmed and humbled by the graciousness of people. I'd personally never been so moved by a news story that I'd made a gift and sent it to that person. The fact that there are people so filled with kindness makes me feel pretty good about whom I'm spending my time with on this planet.

A bit after Jack's run, I tried my best to readapt to work. Just as I was about to dive into one of several files, my secretary beeped in to tell me that an assistant with Senator Deb Fischer of Nebraska's office was on the phone. After the call was connected, I was informed that Senator Fischer would be introducing a resolution on the floor—a resolution that declared September 26th—national pediatric brain cancer awareness day in honor of Jack Hoffman.

Finally. Our message was getting somewhere. This was exactly what we needed. The federal government was the top spender on cancer research in America. We needed them on our team.

After working through the details with the staff assistant, I asked if I might be able to visit with Senator Fischer. The staff assistant obliged. A few hours later, Senator Fischer called me to discuss the resolution, among other things.

During our discussion, the Senator told me that President Barack Obama knew about Jack's fight and his touchdown run. She said that, at a recent meeting, she'd handed a Nebraska newspaper clip to President Obama. He made a comment about the Hoffmans coming to the White House for a visit. She asked if we'd consider it, and I replied with a resounding yes.

A few days later, Senator Fischer called to schedule our visit with the President. I asked who to call.

"Andy, I don't have a number," she said. "Just call the White House; they're expecting to hear from you."

I thought to myself, *well, this isn't going anywhere.*

I used Google to find any kind of number.

"White House operator," the voice on the other end of the line said.

"Yes, hello—my name is Andy Hoffman," I said sheepishly. "I was told to call the White House to schedule a meeting with President Obama."

She pressed me for details. I explained the connection with Senator Fischer. I told her about Jack's televised touchdown. As I spoke, I felt absurd. When I was done talking, she placed me on hold. After waiting for approximately five minutes, I was transferred to a new person.

"Hi, this is Anita Decker," the new voice stated.

From my desk in my rural law practice office in the middle of a cow pasture in Nebraska, I spoke to the personal assistant of President Obama. We started talking dates, and immediately realized how difficult scheduling our visit would be.

"This is where it gets kind of dicey," said Anita. "I will just tell you what dates and times are open, and you have to tell me which one works for you."

While she was very pleasant, her voice made it clear that she had scheduled thousands of meetings for the President. We were happy to be flexible. The only thing we requested was that all five of our family members could attend—and, of course, our favorite Husker, Rex Burkhead. Anita agreed to the request.

After the meeting was scheduled, Ms. Decker and I had a chat about what my family should wear and what to expect at the White House. I heard someone in the background yell, "Yo!"

Ms. Decker chuckled and said, "That was the President."

The visit to the White House was scheduled for April 29th, nearly three weeks after the run. It was a good opportunity to see my sister, who lived in Clarksburg, Maryland. She was a government contractor and quite familiar with the Beltway. After we landed in D.C., my sister picked us up at the airport and took us to her house for a debriefing. After some laughs and several beers, we were officially ready for the next morning.

Rex, on the other hand, was coming in from Dallas. He'd been drafted two days prior. He held a draft celebration the night before his flight.

Upon our arrival at the White House, we had to go through security. Even though we filed through security with a newly drafted NFL running back, the guards took more notice of Jack. They even took pictures with him; they were so excited to meet the boy who'd scored that touchdown.

We then made our way to the White House waiting room. While I used the restroom, my family was instructed to not have their cell phones out around the President. Being the compliant Midwesterners that my wife and children were, they didn't dream of breaking the rule.

Not knowing the regulations, I walked out of the bathroom, cell phone in hand, getting ready to take a picture. From across the room my wife softly yelled, "Put your phone away!"

We sat next to individuals in snappy attire who looked like they were with the FBI or some high level military brass. The waiting room displayed stately wall hangings and portraits of sophisticated people.

We anxiously waited for the call. I was still in shock that we were even there.

"Take a good look around, kids, because you are never going to be in this room again," said my wife.

"That's not necessarily true," remarked a smiling gentleman sitting across the room. "Any one of them could be president someday."

Interesting thought.

Bri smiled back and replied, "I guess you're right."

Our nerves tingled. Suddenly, a polite (but assertive) woman opened the door. She looked at our family and said, "The President will see you now."

Should I advocate for pediatric brain cancer research? Should I try to explain to him why the disease was the worst possible illness a child could get? I didn't want to waste this priceless opportunity.

Together, we walked toward the back of the Oval Office.

President Obama met us at the door.

He immediately handed Jack a football with his signature on it. He then presented all of our children with gift bags full of playing cards (with pictures of the White House dog on them), White House M&Ms, and other goodies. My wife and I tried to remain normal, despite the fantastical situation.

President Obama was amazing to our family. In that moment with us, he wasn't distracted by aides, calls, or memos. One hundred percent of his attention was ours.

We walked toward the Oval Office desk. The President sat on the edge of the desk, and we all gathered around him. President Obama guided our conversation with seamless ease; if any of us spoke, it was because he allowed it. He wasn't one bit rude—quite the opposite—but he held command over the visit.

After making basic acquaintances, the President looked at Rex and acknowledged the recent draft: "Cincinnati Bengals." He held a gaze with Rex and then commented, "So, what happens next?... Never mind, I know what happens next."

Did Obama ever play football? How does he know what Rex is in for? My brain raced.

"I watched Hard Knocks on HBO," the President said playfully.

We couldn't help but giggle.

President Obama then told us about a new brain science project that he was working on with a number of scientists from all over the world. He was excited about the brain mapping aspect of the project and its potential to help pediatric brain cancer patients. We discussed how that could lead to many more discoveries.

In the end, however, my message to President Obama was one of simplicity. I told him, "Thank you for allowing us the opportunity to meet you. The opportunity to have this visit, in and of itself, was a tremendous gift for us to raise awareness for pediatric brain cancer. Your seeing us will help save lives."

I spoke as a father, on the brink of tears, to another father. His face was sincere.

As we prepared to leave, President Obama hugged our children and shook my and Rex's hand. Bri moved in to shake his hand as well, but he stopped her. The President opened up his arms and said, "We hug moms."

That was one of the coolest things I had ever seen. Such a kind and gentle soul.

My family filed out of the Oval Office, and I was the entourage's caboose. I made it to just outside the doorway when I heard President Obama rise from the desk and step toward me.

"Hey, Andy—hold up a second," the President said. I froze.

He looked right at me and said, "If you see Senator Fischer, please be sure to thank her for this. She had a lot to do with it."

I told him that I appreciated his gratitude toward her. And just like that, our fifteen-minute White House visit was over.

We then went outside and took a few more pictures around the White House before walking a few blocks to get something to eat and decompress. We talked with much laughter between our words.

I received a text from Ms. Anita Decker. She asked to use one of their official pictures of the President and Jack as their White House photo of the day. After discussing that with Bri, we obliged. The next morning, the photo was on the front page of the *Omaha World Herald* and the front page of the *USA Today* sports section.

What a trip.

Chapter Twenty

ESPYS!

We were exhausted when we got back to Nebraska. Shortly after landing in Omaha, we were greeted by a television interviewer. When we stopped at a gas station, we saw Jack on the front page of the *Omaha World-Herald* for the first time. All of the notoriety was overwhelming. We felt unworthy of the attention.

Being back in Atkinson was nice. There, we were simply the Hoffmans. Nothing fancy or flashy. Just everyday hardworking Americans.

We thought things would begin to slow down in May. That certainly did not happen.

A number of former Huskers athletes and celebrities, including Ndamukong Suh, Lindsey Moore, Alex Gordon, Larry the Cable Guy, Alex Henery, and Bo Pelini lent their names to our t-shirts to help the cause. And by July of that year, we'd sold nearly eight hundred thousand dollars of Team Jack gear. We could barely believe it.

Our family assumed the ride was coming to an end. As the sun set on the month of May, we looked forward to a summer full of t-ball and chasing the kids around the lake. It was time to be normal human beings again. (Yet again, so we thought.)

On a warm and sunny day in early June, I received a telephone call from an ESPN producer. They informed me that they'd selected Jack's touchdown run as a finalist for the 2013 ESPY's best moment award.

Over the next forty-five days, our family was again subjected to a torrent of media interest in Jack's life. He was to travel to Los Angeles to go up against Alex Morgan and Indianapolis Colts Head Coach Chuck Pagano for the award. This entire experience was becoming unfathomable.

My wife and I once again questioned whether we were doing the right thing. We certainly did not want to draw an overabundance of attention to ourselves and our family. After all, you don't move to a town without stoplights because you want national attention. This was pretty much the opposite of what we'd envisioned for our lives.

Again, we embraced it in order to continue spreading our critical message. We decided to press forward, as we'd already gotten that far…and in our minds, it was too late to turn back.

Our family had grown much tighter through Jack's cancer journey. It further cemented my wife's belief that family was always paramount. Our family didn't split—we'd all been in Omaha for that thirty days, we'd all been in Boston for that other thirty days. Thus, when Jack was called to Los Angeles, it became our family call. Where Jack went, we all went. Bri was vehement about it. She stated, "If we are going to California, Andy, we are taking the girls. And we're going to go to Disneyland. Otherwise we don't go at all." My wife couldn't have cared less about the ESPYs and its pageantry. Heck, until Jack was nominated, she had never even heard of the ESPYs.

Our ESPN contact had assumed that only Jack, Jack's parents, and Rex Burkhead would be attending the event. Our taking the girls could've presented a problem. Reese was only three at the time, and Ava was only five. For anyone who's watched the ESPYs, you know there aren't too many toddlers in the audience.

The problem was easily solved by taking a babysitter with us on the trip. My freshly graduated niece, Samantha Hoffman, fit the bill perfectly. Then, the next thing we needed to do is line up Disney tickets—and ESPN was all over it. Whatever the Hoffman family needed, ESPN would provide it. They made us feel like royalty. They handed us six roundtrip plane tickets and six three-day passes to

Disneyland. It seemed as though it would be the trip of a lifetime… and it absolutely was.

Bri and I stared at each other when we learned the ESPYs were preceded by a red carpet appearance. Red carpet? Who the hell goes from a small Nebraska town to the red carpet?

Well…Bri needed a dress.

The story behind Bri's ESPYs dress started in Boyd County, Nebraska (county population of twenty-one hundred). During my high school years in Spencer, I became good friends with a kid from a Butte High School sports team. His name was Joey Hausmann. We were good enough friends, in fact, that I was his wingman on his first date with his future wife. (My night didn't end with a kiss, though.) Joey went on to marry Rebecca, who would tragically die of cancer over twenty years later. Rebecca's brothers, Matt and Adam, played for the Huskers as walk-ons. In Nebraska, Joey was well-known for starting the very successful Hausmann Construction company. I am grateful for his friendship to this day.

What people may not have known about Joey was that he had a younger sister by the name of Jennifer Hausmann. Jennifer was a fashion designer in Los Angeles at the time. What were the chances? A local Boyd County girl was in L.A., hanging out with red carpet regulars. She was in the midst of launching her own clothing line (which centered around denim pieces), and she offered to outfit Bri for the ESPYs.

However, therein lay the catch: Bri's dress was to be denim. A denim dress on the red carpet? But we were just bold enough—and rural enough—to think it was an excellent idea.

Jennifer made the dress, came to The Ritz Carlton in downtown Los Angeles the day before the ESPYs, and fitted the dress perfectly for my wife. Bri had only ever looked more beautiful on our wedding day. Jennifer's work was outstanding. It was yet another example of a Nebraskan helping a Nebraskan.

My parents and some friends came to join us in L.A. Rex was unable to accept his invitation to the ESPYs due to his Cincinnati Bengals commitments, so they then asked Taylor Martinez to appear instead. The day before the event, Taylor arrived at our hotel and hung out with us around the time Bri was in her dress fitting.

We asked Taylor what he planned to wear. He said that he was just going to wear a shirt and slacks. I strongly encouraged him to consider a shirt and tie, which, apparently, he didn't even own. At that point, Jennifer said, "Taylor, let's go shopping."

So, Jennifer and Taylor hit the best shops in downtown L.A.—and she knew the best. In short, Jennifer outfitted nearly everyone from Nebraska for the 2013 ESPYs.

The hotel bustled with sports stars the day before the event—J.J. Watt, Stuart Scott, Adrian Peterson, and many others. We also rubbed elbows with virtually every ESPN star imaginable, from Chris Berman to Stephen A. Smith. It was quite a scene.

Jack's visit with Stuart Scott was most memorable. While chilling in the ESPYs lounge, we sat beside Stuart, upon his invitation. He had all kinds of questions for Jack: "How is chemo going?" "Do you throw up after chemo?"

He then asked Jack where his port was. Jack lifted his shirt to show Stuart where his needle was inserted. Stuart then lifted up his shirt and showed Jack his own port. Stuart spoke to Jack with great encouragement, and Jack spoke to Stuart like he was a big brother. Stuart's personality was infectious. The world is a better place for having hosted him.

The night of the ESPYs, we stepped out of a black SUV and were escorted to the Staples Center. Suddenly, we were on the red carpet.

What an experience.

To this day, there are Getty Images of our family and Taylor Martinez slowly making our way down the red runner.

While waiting to enter the venue, we occupied our time by visiting with Dwyane Wade, Johnny Manziel, and Taylor. We gave each of them a Team Jack wristband, told them about pediatric brain cancer, and the great need for funding. Dwyane put his wristband on—and later Tweeted a photo of it. He singlehandedly had Team Jack trending on Twitter that night.

After the doors opened, our niece and two daughters veered off the red carpet to enjoy pizza and the TV coverage back at the hotel.

We headed for our seats.

Before sitting down, Jack and I broke away for a restroom break. On our way there, we met none other than Mr. Belding from *Saved by the Bell*. The surprises just kept coming.

Our seats were placed near the front, two rows behind Snoop Dogg. Because we'd been engulfed in Jack's journey for so long, we'd forgotten about celebrities. Taylor had to remind us who people were, as we were essentially clueless. But we definitely recognized Chris Connelly, who'd witnessed our overstuffed basement.

Before everything started, we were told by one of the assistant producers that they would come and find us two commercial breaks before the award was presented. They would then put a mic on Jack—"Just in case." Being the only guest under five feet tall, if he won, Jack wouldn't be able to reach the microphone.

Of course, they knew full well that Jack was going to win. However, we did not know this was "just in case."

The event began, and we sat there with butterflies the entire time. It was definitely difficult to get comfortable in the chair, knowing that we could shortly be up in front of five thousand guests and another two or three million viewers. Back home, our family (and a good chunk of Nebraska) stared at the TV. We definitely felt the pressure.

Two commercial breaks prior to the best moment award came and went, but we saw no producer. More awards were handed out. Then, it was announced there would be a commercial break…with the best moment award presentation to immediately follow.

About that time, a frantic young assistant scrambled up to us and said, "I couldn't find you."

I laughed and replied, "We've been here the whole time!"

The assistant then wired us up and wished us luck.

Moments later, Jack and I nervously watched the best moment of the year candidates' introductions. I will never forget watching my son's highlight and listening to "I Lived" by OneRepublic. I frequently find my mind treading back to that moment in time, as if it were a dream.

Tate Donovan and Kerri Walsh Jennings came out to introduce the award. The music stopped; the crowd was completely silent and still.

"And the ESPY goes to…" Tate began, "…Jack Hoffman!"

Jack and I, totally wide-eyed, then went up on stage. Everything we said probably seemed unrehearsed, but it had been heavily prepared. While I absolutely made sure to say "pediatric brain cancer," I also wanted to thank the two men who'd gotten us on that stage—Rex Burkhead and Coach Pelini.

Then we were rushed off to backstage. We took selfies with Tate and Kerri. I realized we were only ten feet from LeBron James. That brought the butterflies back.

There were several studios set up in the backstage area. One was for *Good Morning America*. While at that studio, we met Josh Elliott. He was delightfully kind and took time to be with us. He put on a Team Jack wristband as we described our mission. That would not be the last time Josh Elliott would interview Jack.

After the event, we were completely swarmed. Person after person rushed to us, asking for a photo with Jack. It was a madhouse. It took us nearly an hour and a half to make it from the venue back to the hotel room. Jack carrying his ESPY award on the streets of L.A. may've had something to do with it.

After a brief stop at the room to celebrate with parents and family, Bri joined Jack and me for a post-ESPYs celebration in the hotel ballroom. More madhouse. More celebrities. So many more stories.

At the party, Jack wandered and found himself a comfy couch in the noisy room. He was hungry, and we had found a bun for him to eat, but his excitement remained. He was still thrilled. As he munched on his bread, Ava and Reese were still up in the room. He reveled in the fact that he was drinking pop and staying up late while his sisters were sleeping. That's what actually excited him the most in that moment, I have no doubt.

A gentleman interrupted me and asked if he could meet Jack.

"You bet," I replied. "But can you come back in a few minutes? He's trying to eat."

While I was still friendly, I didn't exude the warmth I usually did back home. I thanked the gentleman and his son for stopping by to say hello. I had no idea who I'd just spoken to.

After the gentlemen walked away, Kenny Bell rushed over to me: "Uhhh, that was Chris Tucker!"

"Are you kidding," I blurted.

Utterly mortified, I reached into Bri's purse and pulled out a Team Jack wristband. Jack and I walked over to Mr. Tucker.

"Here—we have a few extra of these," I said politely. "Jack would like you to have one."

Genuinely sincere, Chris thanked Jack for the wristband. In an apologetic tone, I then asked Chris and his son if we could take a photo of Jack with them.

After I snapped my own picture, Chris gave me his phone so that I could capture one for him, too.

I shook Chris' hand and Jack gave him a high-five.

"Thank you so very much," Chris said. "This is so great. Thank you."

I found it quite telling of his character that even after I'd snubbed him, he treated my son and I like a million bucks.

I thanked Kenny Bell for helping me put names to the surrounding faces—and then I continued leaning on his expertise.

He then pointed subtly to an athletic woman who looked vaguely familiar. "That's Lolo Jones," he said, eyes wide and jaw hanging. "She's one of the greatest female hurdlers of all time."

"Come on, Jack," I said. "Grab some wristbands."

Another visit and round of photos later, Jack's photo album neared completion. I was thrilled at so many opportunities to spread the Team Jack word.

Jack made it for another hour before calling it quits.

As we entered the lobby, the crowd burst into applause and cheers for Jack. He gazed around as we walked through the smiling faces.

"Dad, can you believe all of those people wanting their picture taken with me?" Jack asked once we were taking off our shoes in the hotel room. "There I was, trying to eat my food, and people kept coming up to me and wanting their picture taken with me." My son raised his eyebrows. "I was, like, 'Geez people, get ahold of yourself.'"

That quip provided much laughter for some time to come.

I returned to the ballroom to join Bri. We also had the company of Jennifer and her assistant Claire Eckstrom, Kenny (and his stepfather, Dan Campbell), and Taylor. We recounted and relived the day together. Accomplishment, support, and inspiration were collaboratively commemorated.

Our visiting was suddenly interrupted (in a very un-Nebraska-like manner) by the disc jockey: "Snoop Dogg is in the motherfucking house!"

Following Kenny and Taylor's lead, we moved closer to the stage. We marveled. I think it maybe started sinking in at that point…we were at a private ESPYs party in L.A., watching an exclusive Snoop Dogg performance.

I looked at Bri. "We're a long way from the farm, Mom."

"This is crazy," Bri replied.

That night would not soon be forgotten.

Our late-night partying nearly cost us our flight back. We were supposed to be picked up at 7:30 a.m. We woke up at 7:10 a.m. Nothing was packed; the room was a disaster. There was absolutely no time to shave or shower. We had an entire day of travel in front of us. We faced a six- to eight-hour flight (counting our connection), and then a four hour drive from Omaha. It was going to be a long day.

Fortunately, we reached our van and made it to the airport in time. On the way to the airport, Scott Poese of our local KBRX Radio station called me for a live interview.

We checked all of our luggage, except one item—the ESPY. We carried it in our arms the entire time, but it got a scratch, which we simply considered a character mark. On our way to airport security, we ran into Linda Cohn of ESPN. We thought for sure she would be our last celebrity of the trip.

We soon learned that we were on the same flight as Taylor, Kenny, and Kenny's stepfather, Dan. It was a fun trip back with those fellows. In Denver, we parted ways. Before saying our goodbyes, we took a group photo that became one of the most memorable shots from our adventure.

Chapter Twenty-One

NOW WHAT?

When I talk about Jack's touchdown run, I find it best to put it this way: the score wasn't for the red team, the white team, or the Huskers—it was for the children whose struggle we'd seen firsthand.

And we were so grateful that the Team Jack Foundation was totally booming. When we returned home from L.A., apparel sales and donations flooded in left and right. By early August, my wife and I began preparing for our first foundation fundraiser.

We'd decided to throw a celebration for National Pediatric Brain Cancer Awareness Day in Atkinson, which, per Senator Fischer's decision, would be on Jack's birthday. We also planned the first-ever Team Jack Radiothon for the same day. At the rate we were moving, I considered giving up my law practice to devote all of my time to volunteering—but it didn't seem right to not add my sweat to the rest of my family's day-to-day efforts. All of my children needed me.

During this Team Jack boom, I learned of a remarkable human being…Dan Gilbert. Never heard of him? Dan signed LeBron James' paychecks while he was in Cleveland. Dan was a real estate developer and owned Quicken Loans. He was a mover and a shaker, a natural entrepreneur. What people don't know, however, was that Dan's son had a brain tumor…and Dan had started his own foundation to fight a specific illness called NF1. Dan used his entrepreneurial skills and business acumen to raise millions of dollars for kids in need. I deeply respected and admired him—an instantaneous role model. Dan showed me that, with enough discipline, I could kick ass raising money to fight a disease and also work hard professionally.

Unfortunately, my wife and I got our first taste of people spreading rumors at that time. The first rumbling actually occurred in a private Facebook message to me on the morning of the ESPYs. Someone had sent me a message on the Team Jack Facebook page asking how we were spending all of the foundation money and if we were "buying land." A few months later, while visiting with a client, he informed me that he'd heard Bri and I were taking the money. That rumor later cropped up again in 2019. One client even told me that his parents did not want to hire me because my family already had plenty of money due to Team Jack.

It was pure garbage. I pitied the people who thought and talked that way.

Those individuals needed to stop and think big for a moment. It was, in fact, possible for us to support our family and still grow the foundation in the evenings and on the weekends. We even found time to go fishing, hunting, and running. What we didn't have time to do, however, was sit around and dream up hateful rumors about people who were trying to change things for the better. I had zero time for such closed-mindedness.

In 2016, my wife and I built a four-thousand-square-foot building that held three offices with separate entrances. One was for the Team Jack headquarters. So, of course, the rumors resurfaced. Zero funding from the foundation had been used to construct the facility, as part of it would be used for my law practice. Both the foundation and my practice were integral in our lives, so it only made sense to have them neighbor each other. Simple minds wasted time imagining otherwise.

As we juggled the foundation and our lives, Bri and I eventually discussed stopping Team Jack altogether. We would hold the awareness day celebration and then just be done. But my gut told me that we had too much momentum going and quitting would be a mistake. We took a risk and sought to hire someone to run the foundation all day, every day.

As we began scouting, several names were provided to us.

One in particular was a young lady who'd graduated from our hometown high school in 2004: Kylie Tielke (later Dockter). Kylie had just returned to Atkinson after having worked for three years in Denver at a children's foundation that raised money to fight cancer and other diseases. She had experience hosting rather large events. Jackpot.

A few days after learning of Kylie's presence in Atkinson, we interviewed her. The next day, we offered her the job. The day after that, she accepted. The rest is history.

To this day, Kylie still runs the Team Jack Foundation. Prior to the pandemic of 2020, the foundation always made more money than the year before. Kylie's outstanding work and direction offered our mission constant growth. At the current moment, she oversees three other full-time employees and has helped the foundation gross over one million dollars for seven years in a row. Her integrity is impeccable. Team Jack annually files a Form 990 and has achieved a Platinum GuideStar Seal of Transparency. Approximately ninety percent of all donations received are allocated to research.

From the moment Kylie was hired in August of 2013, she had forty-five days to help us organize and throw one of the biggest parties that Atkinson had ever hosted.

And, oh—what a celebration it was.

We sold out the Atkinson Community Center. The Huskers truck, which hauled the athletes' gear for away games, came to Atkinson for the event. Monte Selden, owner of the Huskers truck, continues to support Team Jack today. Eric Crouch flew in as a guest speaker. Assistant Football Coach Jeff Jamrog also flew in to speak. The Governor of Nebraska traveled to join us. Brain cancer families from across the state came to participate. And one of the most memorable guests of the night was a friend I'd made at the EPSYs: Dan Campbell. Dan showed up that night, all the way from Denver, bearing a gift of twenty-five thousand dollars for the foundation.

After the radiothon and every other festivity, we'd raised two hundred fifty thousand dollars for childhood brain cancer research.

To date, we have yet to repeat a fundraiser of that caliber in Atkinson. However, a few short months later, the Team Jack Foundation held its first gala at the Lincoln Marriott Cornhusker Hotel. This event also sold out. The Annual Team Jack Gala has occurred each year since then…and it always sells out. These gatherings have had the privilege of hosting speakers like Bo Pelini, Jim Kelly, Scott Hamilton, Eric Berry, Amy Robach, Mark Herzlich, and Tom Osborne.

Without question, Jack's touchdown run did far more for fighting pediatric brain cancer than it did personally for Jack and our family. We'd committed to use any offered avenue to spread the word. We never ever lost clear sight of our mission.

I am proud of how we, as a family, achieved that. I'm proud of how everyone on Team Jack achieved that.

In late September of 2013, I received a call from Fox News in New York City. I shook my head, unable to believe this was still happening. On the other end of the line was the producer for *Fox & Friends*. Elisabeth Hasselbeck and her cohosts requested that Jack and I travel to New York and appear live on the show.

Our family had taken a hell of a lot of trips in 2013. We were wiped. After discussing this one with Bri in depth, I called the producer back and told her we'd be there—with one stipulation.

"Jack and I will be glad to fly out and be on the show," I said on the phone. "However, you must promise us that we'll have no less than a full sixty seconds to talk about pediatric brain cancer and the urgent need for research funding."

The producer hesitated. I immediately assumed she was going to pull the plug.

"I cannot guarantee that," she started responding. "I'll have to talk to my senior producer and let you know if that's even possible. I've never had anybody ask this."

She called back five minutes later: "We will give you the time that you want to talk about pediatric brain cancer."

Sure enough, during our *Fox & Friends* appearance in early October of 2013—after going through the usual feel good stuff—

Elisabeth Hasselbeck looked right at me and said, "Andy, I understand there is something that you would like to tell people about pediatric brain cancer." I took that opportunity to take another swing at the disease.

Remarkably, a thousand dollars was donated online from Louisiana soon after I made the public plea.

After our interview, Elisabeth Hasselbeck visited with Jack and me for almost an hour in the greenroom. She wanted to learn more about the disease—and specifically why there was so little funding.

We were always pumped that our media appearances gave funds to cancer research, but we were equally thrilled that they spread awareness. And very early on in the process, I learned that awareness directly equated to education about the disease, which then created research dollars. America knew very little about this disease, and we did our part—every chance we could—to scream from the mountaintops about how much pain the disease caused. We didn't know it at the time, but Team Jack's brand was being born…and it was a brand that existed only to help children like Jack.

After *Fox & Friends*, Jack was invited to St. Louis, Missouri, for the Musial Awards, named after baseball Hall of Famer Stan Musial. There, my son accepted a sportsmanship award on behalf of the Nebraska Cornhuskers football team. We were beyond humbled and honored to be included in such a respectable, outstanding event—as a full family, of course.

Jack was then invited to attend a fundraiser in Philadelphia for the Michael's Way nonprofit cancer foundation. They wanted to share Jack's story as a source of inspiration—but also as a source to inspire giving. They also wanted to present Jack with a Michael's Way Hero Award. The event also involved the Philadelphia Eagles, and many players were in attendance.

Former Eagles Head Coach Dick Vermeil spoke that evening. He shed tears while speaking, and the room was right there with him. That man was all heart—admirably so.

When Jack was introduced in the program, they played his ESPN story in full. Then he was presented the award. Jerry Rice then took to the stage to deliver his speech—but before he even started, he looked directly at our table and said, "Jack Hoffman, you are my hero."

That one left an impression. A three-time Super Bowl champion called my son his hero. And he meant it.

On that trip, we captured Jerry Rice's autograph on a mini helmet to sell for cancer research money.

Each trip was, regardless of fond memories, a work trip. It was God's work.

Including medical trips to Boston, Jack took eight airplane rides in 2013. We had to quickly learn how to be efficient travelers. Certainly, things would slow down in 2014. They needed to. We had bills to pay. We also needed some semblance of normalcy.

In early 2014, we learned that Dan Whitney, also known as Larry the Cable Guy, volunteered to hold a fundraiser for the Team Jack Foundation in Lincoln. It was scheduled for late April at the Pinnacle Bank Arena—only sixty days after our first Team Jack Gala. Now, all of a sudden, the first quarter of 2014 was nuts.

The first gala raised over three hundred thousand dollars—an epic success. We then turned our attention to the Larry the Cable Guy concert.

In our private conversations with Mr. Whitney prior to the show, he let us in on a little secret. He was going to surprise the folks in Lincoln with a guest appearance by Jeff Foxworthy. What an amazing night it was. With nearly ten thousand people in attendance, close to two hundred thousand dollars was raised by the two stand-up comics.

Following the comedy event, Jack and I traveled to Sarasota, Florida, to meet Dick Vitale and attend his gala. Jack and Bo Pelini were Dick's special guests. The Dick Vitale Gala was a must-see event—and still is. Over nine hundred people attended that night, and it felt as grand as the ESPYs. All of the money raised at the gala went to the V Foundation for Cancer Research specifically for pediatric cancer.

At this particular Gala, Dick Vitale had big plans. He was going to have Jack and Bo come up on stage and talk about the run. John Saunders would interview Jack and Bo. Jack and I flew in the night before, and very uncharacteristically, Bri had to stay behind due to an immovable scheduling conflict.

The next day, as Jack and I were getting ready to leave for the gala, I received a phone call from Bo.

"Hey, Andy," he said. "I'm stuck in Atlanta. My flight got delayed. I won't make it. I'm so sorry."

I told Coach Bo that the Vitale camp had been checking with me to see what his status was.

"Tell them I'm sorry, but there's just nothing I can do," Bo replied.

"Coach," I countered, "I'm going to check in with them. I will call you right back. Something tells me they will figure out a way to get you down here."

As Coach Bo was trying to avoid spending the entire night in Atlanta, I spoke to the gala coordinators. They were distraught over the possibility of Coach Bo not making it. As I reflect, I completely understand their angst. We would have travel issues with our foundation's gala speakers in the future.

Coach Bo and the gala coordinators got connected. The Vitale camp had lined up a private jet to take Coach Bo from Atlanta to Sarasota. Problem solved.

Before the gala, we had a press conference behind closed doors. We stood and visited with Nick Saban during that time, which was an incredible honor. Later that night, Coach Saban won me over even more. As donations were being solicited from the crowd, Coach Saban donated fifty thousand dollars for cancer research. Incredible.

At supper that night, Coach Bo, Jack, and I sat with Jimbo Fischer. We all enjoyed the time away from the pressure and the media.

Coming away from the Dick Vitale event in 2014, I was even more driven as a human being to raise money and awareness for child brain cancer research. After having been to the ESPYs and the V Foundation fundraiser, I became convinced that those folks were some of America's finest.

What was so remarkable about Mr. Vitale was that he'd never had a child diagnosed with cancer. Yet, there he was, making the entire crowd cry as he described a child going through chemotherapy or radiation. His dramatic tone and storytelling ability raised millions of dollars for those kids, and still does. We were so sad when Dick couldn't make it to our 2019 Team Jack Gala, but we couldn't stop a snowstorm, unfortunately. To this day, Mr. Vitale is a good friend— and he frequently calls or texts to check on Jack. Whenever he sees a news clip about Jack, he sends a text to let us know our son is in his prayers.

On one occasion, there was a national news update on a medical treatment that Jack was then taking. Mr. Vitale called, nearly on the edge of tears.

"Andy, what's going on with my main man, Jack?" he managed. "Is he going to be okay? Please, tell me he's going to be okay."

This man is a blessing to mankind. He is somebody that I hold in the highest possible regard.

Once we returned from Florida, things—finally—started to slow. By the end of 2014, life had almost become normal again… which was good, because in March of 2015, I left my law practice and started my own law firm. Honestly, I made the move because I'd become such a lousy law partner. I had to be everywhere at once, and that didn't make for a good law team.

That's when we decided to construct our three-office facility in Atkinson. As I previously explained, it gave progress to the foundation and my career, not to mention it was clearly more efficient. I loved the opportunity to visit the Team Jack staff and spitball ideas with them regularly. Building our purpose and mission was (and remains) my inextinguishable fire.

Chapter Twenty-Two
PERSONALLY INSPIRED

Back in 2013, some folks at the Boston Children's Hospital had discussed the 2014 Boston Marathon with me. They wanted me to consider being a charity runner for their hospital. Having just recently taken up running, I told them I would think about it. After discussing it with Bri, I let them know I was in.

I utilized the Boston Children's Hospital personal trainer and religiously used his program as my training guide. I knew that I wasn't a natural runner; my family was known for our bullheadedness and toughness on the gridiron—and being a hair on the short side, compared to some. Even though I was a decent football player in my own right (like my kin), jogging wasn't a similar experience. But I have to say, there's nothing quite like taking a long run on Nebraska's abandoned railroad Cowboy Trail in the dead of winter.

I ran my first half marathon in October of 2013. I'd lost eighty-five pounds while training for it, after many years of wanting to get in better shape. By April of 2014, I felt a bit more prepared for the Boston Marathon.

Truthfully, Jack was my inspiration to get healthier and start running. There I was, asking him to be strong and physically persevere—while, frankly, I looked like I'd let myself go. What kind of example was I setting for him? Jack's courageous fight became my inspiration in many ways.

Funnily enough, when we'd been back in Boston in 2012 for a few of Jack's medical checkups, we'd gone to the top of the Prudential Center Tower downtown. There were binoculars that we could stick a quarter into so we could see the sights. I gazed at everything from MIT to the Bunker Hill Memorial Bridge. At one point, I spotted the finish line for the Boston Marathon on Boylston Street, right in front of the library.

I commented to my wife, "Who in the hell would wanna run that?"

Two years later, I found out.

Even though my race time ended up being far from stellar (remember, I'm an offensive lineman), running alongside the Boston Children's Hospital team was incredibly inspiring. On the Saturday before the marathon, I had addressed all the runners and their families in front of a thousand people. I told them why I was running for Boston Children's Hospital. In all of my public speaking experiences, that was—hands down—the most emotional I'd ever been. I shared with them what Boston Children's meant to my family and me: at that point, Jack was unequivocally alive thanks to that hospital.

As we waited near the starting line before the marathon, I met an individual by the name of Mark Minichiello. Mark informed me that he was in the process of prepping for another marathon; the Boston Marathon was essentially training for him. He then told me that he lived in Los Angeles but was a Boston native who was running his first Boston Marathon. I shared my story with Mark and told him why I was running. I also told him that on that particular day, I'd selected twenty-six different kids to run in honor of. I told him their names.

Those children were members of the Team Jack family. I dedicated each mile to a different child.

Back home in Nebraska, Lindsey Nemetz of the Team Jack staff tracked my marathon progress. She would post photographs of each child that each mile was dedicated to in real time. Approximately two thousand miles away, I would think about that child and his or her fight as I ran.

It was an emotional day.

That night, as I was going through Facebook, I was a wreck. The families were overwhelmed that I had dedicated a mile to each of their children. It was the least I could do. Those kids inspired me to do the unthinkable—run a marathon.

Mark, from L.A., had offered to pace the race with me and help me finish. At the conclusion of the race, before we parted ways, I vowed to Mark that I would run with him again someday.

In 2015, I kept my word. I flew to Los Angeles to run the L.A. Marathon with him. Then, in October of 2015, I ran the Chicago Marathon and we shared time together at the starting line.

My next two marathons were in Minneapolis in 2016 and 2017. The 2017 marathon was one of my most rewarding, as I had the privilege of running alongside my wife. It was her first marathon— and she crushed my first marathon time by nearly twenty minutes. I was so proud of her.

For me, the best thing about marathons was that it felt like each step I took was progress; each of my exhausted breaths helped a child. It felt like Jack was there with me, challenging me to a footrace. It further cemented for me that there was no justification for living an unhealthy life; I owed it to myself—and more importantly—my children. If Jack could keep going, so could I. I'd found something deep inside that helped pace me. There were no excuses.

At every marathon, I always handed out Team Jack bracelets to anyone possible, told everyone about my son, spoke about research funding, and proudly donned my Team Jack running singlet. Sure, the races helped me get and stay healthy, but they were always work trips. Our mission couldn't take vacations.

On March 3rd, 2020, I ran the L.A. Marathon again—right before the COVID-19 pandemic struck. It was probably my last marathon...but I'd said that before the previous two marathons.

Who knows.

Chapter Twenty-Three
NASCAR JOINS THE FIGHT

Since the beginning of Jack's journey in April of 2011, we have met so many people. To this day, when we meet a new person, I ask myself, *why did God want us to meet?* Everything seemed to always line up. Nothing seemed an accident.

Jeff Hanson was certainly one of those people. That kid is truly inspiring. In February of 2016, our family had the honor of meeting Jeff and his family at the Team Jack Gala in Lincoln. Jeff, visually impaired due to a brain tumor, is an award-winning painter who has sold pieces to people like Elton John and Danica Patrick. His work is absolutely brilliant. When we met him, he was donating a painting as an auction item for the gala.

Jeff's work helped us blow the roof off the hotel in Lincoln—fifty-four thousand dollars for child brain cancer research. Jim Kelly, the guest speaker that night, purchased a bowtie Jeff created for no less than two thousand dollars. It was unforgettable.

Jeff's parents, Hal and Julie Hanson, spoke with Team Jack volunteer Marilyn Mecham that night. They discussed The NASCAR Foundation's Betty Jane France Humanitarian Award, that was given out each year to one dedicated NASCAR fan who has made an impact on children. The NASCAR Foundation would then award one hundred thousand dollars to the charity the winner represents. Jeff had won it the year before, and Julie was excited to do all she could to get Team Jack involved.

A few days later, Marilyn Mecham nominated me for the Betty Jane France Humanitarian Award. While I have always been a fan of NASCAR, I was not what you would call a die-hard. I'd taken a real liking to Jeff Gordon due to his support for childhood cancer research. I also had fond memories of visiting NASCAR racetracks when I was a kid and, more recently, Charlotte Motor Speedway.

The nomination, which was originally made as an afterthought on the day of the deadline, wasn't supposed to go anywhere. To my surprise, I was announced as a finalist on NASCAR's NBC feature show in late summer of 2016.

By that point, the Team Jack Foundation was four years old and an unbelievably well-oiled machine. We got to work instantly. An online voting mechanism would decide the winner of the award. With our mailing list of over seventy thousand people, email list of nearly forty thousand people, and a very strong social media influence, the Team Jack Foundation was carried to victory.

That fall, our family attended The NASCAR Foundation Gala at the New York Marriott Marquis in Times Square. At this event, Hoda Kotb from NBC gave the opening remarks and Sara Bareilles sang. Our story was introduced by the NASCAR champion Martin Truex, Jr. We met countless celebrities, and it was like the ESPYs all over again.

Amazingly, I won the award that night. I was entirely overwhelmed by such a celebration for our four years of hard work. The best part of the night was having my entire family there for the event. I would not have wanted it any other way.

As a result of winning the award, I was invited to attend the NASCAR Cup Series Awards in Las Vegas in December of 2016. With Bri as our guidepost, we would only go to Vegas if we went as a whole family.

This event was a terrific opportunity to rub elbows with some of NASCAR's finest racers and raise awareness. Before the NASCAR Cup Awards, we had a one-on-one conference with Jimmie Johnson. During this session, I was able to share with him information about the Team Jack Foundation and its mission. I was also able to encourage him to use his platform to do more good.

We also spent time with Kyle Bush, Tony Stewart, and countless other NASCAR drivers. Perhaps the most exciting part of the night for me was meeting Eddie Vedder of Pearl Jam. As a retirement gift to Tony Stewart, Vedder made a guest appearance. While Vedder was supposed to be the surprise, Tony Stewart and his friends surprised Mr. Vedder in reverse. They presented his foundation with over one million dollars from NASCAR drivers and owners. Vedder and his wife are extremely philanthropic and raise money for a rare disease known as epidermolysis bullosa, a horrible skin disorder. As I was taking my photo with Mr. Vedder, he graciously took a few minutes to let me tell him about the Team Jack Foundation.

The NASCAR event was rewarding on so many levels. Not only was it a fantastic personal experience, but I met someone that I would consider to be a very good personal friend—Rick Allen. Rick was NBC Sports' NASCAR announcer. To this day, Rick emcees the Team Jack Gala every year. He's an integral part of our foundation. Though he was originally from Grand Island, Rick was a Huskers track athlete at Nebraska. I was so grateful, on so many levels, for the Betty Jane France Humanitarian Award experience.

Additionally, while in Las Vegas, we became friends with Pat Warren of Kansas Speedway. Annually, Pat donates an amazing getaway travel package to his racetrack in Kansas City, Kansas. His package routinely fetches anywhere from four to six thousand dollars at our foundation gala. His donations have helped us raise over twenty thousand dollars. Mr. Warren embodies what NASCAR is all about.

From the outside looking in, it probably appeared as though we were just running around the country, rubbing elbows with celebrities, and trying to look important. But we knew how much work each event was…we always had to roll up our sleeves, take a breath, and dive in. The relationships we started would turn into friendships. In turn, these new friends joined our fight against child brain cancer—and not to get their name in the bright lights. It was because they were good and honorable people. God has so richly blessed us with new friends who have made such a gigantic impact on our race for a cure.

Due to the Team Jack Foundation's relationship with The NASCAR Foundation and those in the racing community, more doors opened. Mark Burch of Mark Burch Motorsports in Lincoln was a Team Jack Foundation supporter from day one. Mark has been able to combine his passion for the foundation and his passion for dirt track racing and utilize it to help kids. Thanks to Mark, David Gravel (the most prolific World of Outlaws Sprint racer that this country may have ever seen) wears a firesuit donning the Team Jack logo. His race car also sports a Team Jack logo. The racing community is incredibly generous. We are grateful for the support of the racing community.

From day one, we have not quite been able to fathom or understand why God has gifted us so many incredible opportunities and blessings. But what I can tell you is this: we have always aspired to do the most good as possible with each and every blessing.

Chapter Twenty-Four

JACK'S BRAIN TUMOR

During our rollercoaster of social events, speaking engagements, galas, and the like, our family had a lot to balance. The most important of which was Jack's health. It was always the core priority over everything and anything else.

After Jack's first sixty-week round of chemotherapy, he was taken off treatment in June of 2013. His last day of chemotherapy was just days before the College World Series. While attending the CWS, the announcers caught wind that Jack was in the stadium—and ESPN then found him in the crowd. He basically couldn't go anywhere without being noticed at that point.

After Jack ended chemo, Bri and I grew nervous. When you have a child on chemotherapy—and it seems to be working—you get anxious when it's over. It's almost like when your child swims without a lifejacket for the first time or gets behind the wheel of a car. It wasn't until three months later, in the fall of 2013, that we learned via an MRI that the tumor had not grown. Jack was officially in remission. Praise the Lord.

So, what did this mean? Well, that old shitty drug he'd taken had potentially destroyed his kidneys but simultaneously killed the tumor. But we just didn't know. So, as parents, we just got back to work and tried to stabilize our family. We worked to find our new "normal"…and not let the brain tumor consume our every thought. But every day, the concern was still there.

You learn to cope and deal with something like that by telling yourself things like, "Let tomorrow worry about itself," or, "Life is the slowest rate at which one can die"—or my personal favorite, "We're all terminal." These expressions frequently get you through those moments wherein you begin to pity yourself.

When Jack's port was removed, there came a sense of finality. Was our son cured? After all, the most recent MRI looked good. Damn good. Very little tumor was shown, if any at all.

All along, we knew that Jack's brain tumor had a particularly nasty genetic mutation: BRAF V600E. It is the same genetic mutation that has been crippling and killing melanoma patients for decades. Melanoma, one of the deadliest forms of adult cancer, oftentimes is caused by a genetic mutation—commonly BRAF V600E.

A genetic mutation is an oncogene. Think of an oncogene like a gas pedal. It is the mechanism that causes a brain tumor to grow. With standard chemotherapy like Carboplatin and Vincristine, the solution is to wipe out the fastest growing cells, including the cancer cells. However, thanks to the melanoma patient population, a new drug had been in the works for several years to provide a targeted drug therapy for BRAF V600E. It was known as Dabrafenib.

This targeted drug therapy was different than standard chemotherapy. Imagine this: if you have a rotten tree in a forest, and you wanted to remove the rotten tree, using the standard chemotherapy approach, you would just start a forest fire (as previously illustrated). You would certainly wipe out the bad tree; however, you would kill all of the other trees, as well. But remember that chainsaw I mentioned? With genetic therapies like Dabrafenib, Jack could have his own chainsaw. This was where cancer therapy was headed at that time.

In August of 2014, we learned that Jack's brain tumor had started growing again. And it was growing quickly. He had to reenter treatment.

We were told that they were enrolling children with brain tumors (and the BRAF V600E mutation) in a new clinical trial to test the aforementioned melanoma drug. We did not hesitate to enroll him through the Dana-Farber Cancer Institute.

So, there we were. Treatment. Again. Jack handled the drug well. After approximately thirteen months of treatment and consulting with top brain cancer doctors, we were told that perhaps we should take a break from the drug to see how Jack's tumor would respond. We knew that with the melanoma patients who'd also been taking Dabrafenib, doctors were seeing reoccurrences after some success with remission. Thus, the researchers at Novartis were in the process of researching a multi-drug therapy to stop reoccurrences. They then began two-drug adult trials (Dabrafenib and Trametinib) for melanoma patients around the same time Jack began his Dabrafenib trial.

The plan was that if the tumor came back in a year, we would then hit it with the second clinical trial.

Jack was on Dabrafenib until approximately November of 2015. Jack went 2016, 2017, and most of 2018 without any more treatment.

But the damn thing came back. Again. And this time, it was angry. In August of 2018, Jack started his third cancer therapy. This time, it was the combo therapy of Dabrafenib and Trametinib.

Jack was actually the first child in the United States of America to enroll in this clinical trial. In fact, after enrolling Jack in the trial at Dana-Farber Cancer Institute (only one of two locations where it was offered at the time), Bri and I attended the International Symposium on Pediatric Neuro-Oncology (ISPNO) in Denver, Colorado. This was the largest pediatric brain tumor convention in the world. Researchers and doctors from all over the globe attended this to talk about research projects, search for funding, and collaborate.

While passing through some of the exhibits, we stumbled upon a Novartis exhibit where they were touting a new clinical trial—the very same combo trial that our son was enrolled in. We stopped and looked at the information. The Novartis doctor running the booth started telling us how excited he was that they recently had a child in Boston enroll in the trial just a week prior. We looked him straight in the eye and said, "That's our son."

The man, nearly moved to tears, asked if he could take a picture with us. He said that this was the first time in his career as a drug representative he'd ever met the family of a trial patient.

As of this publication, Jack is still on this clinical trial. While the trial will not entirely erase his brain tumor, we hope that it will stop it in its tracks and kill it. It is time. This is what we pray for several times a day.

Perhaps just as disconcerting about Jack's health is that he is an epileptic. Because a brain tumor is in the center of all function—where a child thinks, breathes, feels, learns, loves, laughs, and plays—it is more than just a cancer. Brain cancer is a lifelong disability due to its location. Jack's tumor is in the seizure part of his brain. Jack takes approximately twenty-two pills a day just to combat his epilepsy. He will likely never drive a car. While he suffers from frequent seizures, they do not tend to be grand mal. His seizures are more like complex partial seizures that cause him to space out for a few minutes at a time. He has experienced these during basketball games and other activities, and they have proven a hardship in his life. He always gets through it, but they are certainly annoying. We have gone to great lengths to try to stop them, from med changes to overnight visitations and monitoring. At some point, Jack may need an operation to not only attempt removing the tumor but also take out some of the seizure focus in his brain.

Despite all of Jack's surgeries, treatments, and medications, he never stops smiling. As a family and as parents, we are not complaining. In fact, we are counting our blessings. We have so much to be thankful for. One of the most rewarding things about the Team Jack project is that we started what is known as the Team Jack Family. This is the group of "brain tumor parents" that support the Team Jack Foundation. Bri and I enjoy the ability to do outreach to other families and provide a support-group setting for them. Many of our friends in this group have lost their children, had their children suffer strokes, or seen their kids unable to walk.

Jack is not a very good poster child for the disease because he is doing so well. He can run, play sports, and terrorize his sisters. Yes, he has seizures. However, in our eyes, he is a normal, pain in the ass boy who does all of the little things that he should.

I am proud of Jack for so many reasons; but the thing that makes me proudest is his stepping out of his comfort zone to talk about his diagnosis and the need for child brain cancer research funding. He truly wants to advocate for other kids and understands the importance of his role. It bothers him that Emma Gehring from Papillion, Nebraska, cannot walk due to a tumor, and Caleb Gulizia has difficulty communicating after several strokes. The struggles that his friends face inspire him to do more. He was placed on earth, in part, to advocate for these kids. All kids.

I would tell any parent with a child diagnosed with a brain tumor that their child does not want to be treated differently. They want to be treated just like everybody else. That is the approach we've always tried to take with Jack. Not only does it make that child's life better and more balanced, it also makes it easier for their siblings to see that there is no special treatment. The reality is, if your child has this diagnosis, they will just automatically receive preferential treatment.

When that child is given an opportunity to score a sixty-nine yard touchdown, win an ESPY, meet the President, have a sports card issued in their honor, and do countless other Forrest-Gump-type things, it becomes even more difficult to raise them. That is why, above all, it has always been so important for us to keep the focus on the Team Jack Foundation's mission of finding research funding.

Jack has a brain tumor. That brain tumor could take his life someday. I hope that it does not. I pray that it doesn't. I pray many times a day that it doesn't.

I am frequently asked, "Andy, why are you so nuts about raising money for child brain cancer research?" That question is usually followed by a mumbling comment like, "…You used to be so normal…"

The truth is that it takes virtually nothing for me to be fired up about the need for child brain cancer research funding. And, in fact, I hope that after reading this, you too will become fired up. What these children have to experience is unfathomable.

Let the following sink in:

There are approximately fifteen thousand three hundred children diagnosed with any form of childhood cancer per year. Of those children, approximately forty-six hundred are diagnosed specifically with pediatric brain cancer. Of those forty-six hundred, one thousand three hundred eighty will not survive. There are nearly one hundred twenty different types and kinds of pediatric brain cancer, making treatment difficult.

With so few children diagnosed with any form of cancer, let alone pediatric brain cancer, there is very minimal incentive for private drug companies to spend money on research and development. You will not find a drug company going out and developing a drug for a disease like neuroblastoma, which affects approximately eight hundred children per year. It just won't happen. Likewise, you will not find a drug company that goes out and tries to develop a drug solely to cure specific types of pediatric brain cancer. Won't happen. Doesn't happen. In fact, there have been seventy-seven new adult cancer therapies developed in the past seven years. Comparatively speaking, there have been just three childhood cancer treatments developed in the past seventy-seven years!

Pediatric physicians are required to take adult drugs, minimize the doses, and give them to kids in hopes they won't kill them. That's the cold hard truth. Yeah, there are laws "requiring" these drug companies to develop drugs with some pediatric benefits and other incentives and such, but it's all garbage.

I understand why a drug company would not invest research dollars with such a low patient population base. When you look at how many people die yearly from melanoma, it makes sense as to why drugs would be perfected for that disease. Drug companies can sell the hell out of it, make a lot of money for the company, and increase the value of their shares. Executives get bonuses and increased pay.

Okay. So, drug companies aren't going to advance research for kids because there's no financial incentive. I can get that. In that case, certainly the government would help us.

Wrong. The federal government wastes more money than you can possibly imagine. While this will not become a federal budget discussion, I think we can all agree that there is a lot of idiotic spending by Uncle Sam. Unfortunately, they—like the drug companies—choose not to spend money on child cancer research. Of all the money that the federal government spends on cancer research, less than four percent of all cancer research dollars are spent on childhood cancer research, let alone childhood brain cancer research. Why? Think about it. Fifteen thousand kids times two parents equals thirty thousand voters. That would hardly win a single precinct in a single election of any kind. These parents are unrepresented in Congress because they have no electoral influence.

I am a Republican. I am a conservative, hardworking, red-blooded American. I drive a pickup. I shoot deer. I am who you probably think I am—a born-and-bred Nebraskan who loves to wash down a steak with a cold beer. But I part ways with my Republican brethren when it comes to childhood cancer research funding. We must enlarge the cancer research pie. When you extrapolate the number of years lost to a child dying of cancer, the loss of life begins to equalize between adults and pediatrics.

Child cancer research is not sexy. Twitter does not get excited about it. Our media does not get excited about it. It is not as inflammatory as some of the other junk that national media covers. So who is to fund this research?

That's where Team Jack comes in. As you can now see, there is a funding gap larger than the Grand Canyon. With the federal government on one side of the canyon and the drug companies on the other, the massive chasm in the middle is where kids go to die. So who's left to fill that gap? Private nonprofits like the Team Jack Foundation. That's who. Plain and simple.

In fact, I will go so far as to say that Jack is still alive today because of private research funding. In 2007, someone donated to

A Kids' Brain Tumor Cure Foundation. They then took that money and invested in research at Harvard's cancer hospital—the Dana-Farber Cancer Institute. Researchers at Harvard then uncovered that some children with brain tumors have a genetic mutation, similar to those seen in adult cancers like melanoma. This research would never have been possible without a private foundation started by a bunch of pissed off parents. My heart always goes out to them and others for fighting the good fight.

Let it be said: America cures the diseases we spend money on. This is not debatable. Think about it. HIV was a death sentence in the 1980s. Today, thanks to research, there are thousands of survivors who will experience full, meaningful lives. In the 1940s, leukemia patients faced a twenty percent chance of survival. Today, due to research advancements, those patients have over a ninety percent chance of survival. The list goes on. The child brain cancer death rate is static; thirty percent of all kids who get a brain tumor will die. This survival rate has not improved in nearly fifty years. Until we spend money on it, real money, this will not change.

Some of the most rewarding experiences that I've had with the Team Jack project have involved sitting in researchers' offices and having them talk about the need for funding. I remember—quite well—a meeting in 2013 with Dr. Mark Kieran, then a pediatric neuro oncologist at Dana-Farber in Boston. During this meeting, Mark was telling me about an exciting new cancer clinical trial that he wanted to start for kids with brain tumors. Unfortunately, he could not get the phone numbers of the big boy cancer foundations (for all of the reasons I just previously mentioned).

He said, "Andy, we need someone to be the first. Will you be the first?"

I told Mark that I would take it back to our scientific advisory board and then let him know. A few days later, I called him back and told him that we would do it; however, we wanted Omaha to be one of the clinical trial sites. While he obliged that request, Omaha was unable to be a trial site. Ultimately, Dr. Kieran took our grant and then got three other foundations to match what we had committed…which helped him launch a 1.2 million dollar clinical trial. The dollars that were used to fund this clinical trial were the same dollars being raised as people went crazy over Jack's touchdown run. When you're fighting child brain cancer, a drop in the bucket has a cumulative effect. Wristbands and t-shirt sales were going to help lead the way in funding a new clinical trial for kids. Then, in 2019, it was quite rewarding when one of the children in our Team Jack Family was actually placed in this clinical trial.

While I understand that our family gets a lot of credit for starting Team Jack and some of these success stories, in the end, it is all due to donors. Generous Nebraskans and people all across the country who have made donations are the reason why a foundation like Team Jack can be successful. It's not because of Jack or our family. It is because of the people that buy books, write checks, attend events, and do everything that they can to help.

Since that first clinical trial investment, we have invested in another clinical trial at Dana-Farber for a new drug known as TAK-580, a DIPG clinical trial at Lurie Children's Hospital of Chicago, a DIPG laboratory research project at Memorial Sloan Kettering Cancer Center in New York, and made a substantial commitment to the University of Nebraska Medical Center at Omaha.

The DIPG project at Memorial Sloan Kettering Cancer Center in New York was for one hundred fifty thousand dollars. After thoroughly vetting the project with our science advisors, the project was recommended for funding. On the day the board approved it, I sent a message to Monica Waggoner—that first Nebraskan "brain cancer mom" I'd ever met, way back in the day—to tell her that Team Jack was donating to fight the kind of brain cancer that her son Nathan had. Unbeknownst to me, it was her birthday. God has a way of providing unexpected rewards. In that case, the reward was mine.

From day one, our goal has been to raise as much money as we can, as fast as we can, and to get that money into the hands of the best researchers in the world. When your son has a brain tumor, you can see early on that the medical objective is to keep him alive long enough for a better treatment to come along. And that's the place we're at in life…along with so many other parents. Trying to keep Jack alive until something better comes along.

Early on, I was routinely asked by well-intentioned Huskers fans: "Why are you investing in research in Boston and not Nebraska?"

My response was simple. Nebraska wasn't selling it. To make my point, I would respond, "The same reason you don't order a pizza at RadioShack. They don't sell brain cancer research here."

I am excited to report that Nebraska is now selling that. And Team Jack is proud to purchase it.

Chapter Twenty-Five

OMAHA!

Jack and I love Nebraska. The Hoffman family, from top to bottom, loves everything about Nebraska. Not just the football team, but the seasons, the people, and the quality of life. Nebraska's greatest natural resource is its people.

While all of Nebraska is great, in particular, I love rural Nebraska. This plays well with my occupation. As a small-town attorney, I enjoy practicing family business law. I take great pleasure in being able to help a family plan for their farm and ranch business estate succession…or a farm wife start an LLC for her new business…the list could go on for miles.

But my love of Nebraska doesn't just begin and end with rural Nebraska. I even enjoy our urban centers, namely Lincoln and Omaha. Lincoln is a cultural mecca, great for concerts, athletic events, and other experiences. Omaha is a medical and business icon for the state. They make Nebraska a stronger, better state.

But in 2011, I could have flushed Omaha down the toilet. I had a very yucky taste in my mouth after the way they'd treated Jack, medically speaking. While the people in Omaha were always very nice, the medical service was horrendous. When we left there and headed to Boston, we took with us a mountain of animosity. After having received center-of-excellence care, we came back to Nebraska with a gigantic chip on our shoulder. We knew that there was a better way to practice medicine when it came to treating children with brain tumors. We saw it. We lived it. We also knew that Omaha was the furthest thing from providing this type of care. In the months that followed our return from Boston, we incessantly choired about how lousy Omaha was at treating kids with brain tumors. We spread the message as broadly as possible.

The vitriol inside me had me doing my absolute best to keep anybody and everybody from treating a medical disease in Omaha. I figured if that was how they treated children with brain tumors, certainly that was how they would treat adults with any kind of disease, as well. Over time, little by little, these sharp pains began to subside.

As the Team Jack Foundation movement began in late 2012 and we started meeting other parents affected by child brain cancer, we soon realized that we were not necessarily like many of these other parents. Yes, it took us a lot of experience and hard lessons, but at that point, we thought critically for ourselves. We were not afraid to challenge medical opinions. We asked the hard questions. And we certainly were not afraid to do things that would uproot an entire family for a month at a time.

While it is hard to admit, we were also unlike other families in that we were blessed with the financial resources to be able to pursue the best treatments in the world. By the time Jack had been diagnosed, my wife and I had lived in Atkinson as a married couple for almost eight years. During this eight-year period, we had done an excellent job of working hard and saving our money. We had resources stockpiled for Jack's diagnosis. God had been preparing us. This is not the norm, however, for most thirty-something parents. Oftentimes, when young parents have a child diagnosed with a brain tumor, things get too tight financially to fly to Boston on a whim.

It took our exposure to a number of other Nebraska families for us to finally realize that not everyone could jump on an airplane to Boston and have the same physicians that Jack had. While we made many referrals for Jack's Boston doctors to other Nebraskans, only four actually had the resources and confidence to make the leap. The majority had no choice but to have their child go through sub-par treatments.

That is why, as I sat there with Harvard's Dr. Mark Kieran and agreed to take his funding request back to my board, I insisted that Nebraska become one of the fifteen clinical trial sites. I was elated when Mark agreed. He understood what I wanted to do—help Nebraska kids have access to better treatments.

I was incredibly disheartened later when he told me that Omaha was unable to host the clinical trial. The University of Nebraska Medical Center and Children's Hospital lacked the infrastructure. It was truly heartbreaking. Here, our Nebraska-based cancer foundation was leading the way with a new treatment, but we couldn't even bring that treatment to our own state for our own kids.

After learning this information, I met with physicians in Omaha to press them on why this was the case. Ultimately, they explained that due to a lack of funding, they were unable to put the resources together to host such a clinical trial. That did not sit right with me. It lit me on fire. Again.

Early in my legal career, I had the opportunity to serve on our local hospital board. This exposed me to rural healthcare from the inside. Bri has spoken at state seminars about her rural pharmacy practice. I have routinely taken an interest in the issues that impact critical-access hospitals like Atkinson. For rural Americans (Nebraskans included), it is all about access to care. And it is likewise just as important for Nebraska kids with brain tumors to have access to care.

In the second full year of the foundation, 2014, I began hearing more and more stories from the front lines. Parents would frequently call me and ask how they could help their child. I kept track of these stories and cases. I kept them in a small journal. In the fall of 2014, the list of stories had grown so long—and seemingly so egregious—that I scheduled an appointment with the Director of Pediatrics at Children's Hospital in Omaha to discuss enhancing pediatric brain cancer care. During this meeting, I gave several examples of horrific treatment stories, much like Jack's. I also shared my discouragement regarding Omaha's inability to host the clinical trial. The administrator reiterated the fact that it was a funding issue.

I followed up that meeting with a phone conference involving the chairperson of the Children's Hospital Omaha board of directors. I was given platitudes and told that she would look into it. Nothing ever developed. The conversation was pointless. I felt disrespected.

I was frustrated about the glaring lack of interest in developing a pediatric brain tumor program in Nebraska. Desperate for action, I went to the state legislature. With the help of my local state legislator (Tyson Larson), we proposed a bill to the state legislature in the winter of 2015. The bill would provide 1.5 million dollars in cancer research funding—if there was a private match by the Team Jack Foundation. Our board enthusiastically agreed.

The funding was to be used for the recruitment of a pediatric neuro-oncologist or other pediatric neuro-oncology specialist. I traveled four hours to Lincoln on multiple occasions to meet with legislators and ultimately testify at a hearing. Then they passed the bill. We got the funding.

Unfortunately, it took nearly two years to recruit the physician the funding had been created for. Institutional politics kept getting in the way. Having grown up in private business, I struggled with the slow bureaucratic processes of large institutions. Regardless, I was a pain in the ass and kept the pressure on. From a private one-on-one meeting with the Chancellor of UNMC, to a phone conference with the Governor, I refused to take my foot off the pedal. There were a lot of department heads to give me the run around. I consistently went to the top and kept singing the company line: this was about kids. That's all. We just wanted to help kids. And not just any kids. Nebraska kids. With brain tumors.

In 2018, we were finally able to get a physician recruited. Unfortunately, the physician ultimately left due to certain political activities surrounding Children's Hospital Omaha. It was a setback that we are continuing to overcome as of the publication of this book.

I am not going anywhere. This project is much too important to give up on.

Over the course of time, our consistent advocacy work has struck a chord. We have become good friends and acquaintances with Chancellor Jeffrey Gold and Dean Brad Britigan at the University of Nebraska Medical Center. We're also working with the director of neurosurgery at UNMC.

After committing the initial 1.5 million dollars to UNMC to match the state legislature's program, the Team Jack Foundation committed an additional five million to UNMC and Children's Hospital Omaha in 2018. This grant was to fund four key areas at UNMC to better the pediatric brain cancer program's development. This program is known as the Power 5. The investment covers the areas of education, clinical and laboratory research, and pain management. We currently have research projects ongoing at the University of Nebraska Medical Center revolving around medulloblastoma and other types of pediatric brain cancer.

While we were excited about our research opportunities at UNMC, our ultimate goal was to help create a center of excellence for children in Nebraska. We believe that our journey and the colleagues we've met along the way can serve as a guiding star in the development of this program. We have availed ourselves on countless times to the UNMC crowd so that we can help develop this program. On multiple occasions, we have assisted in getting Harvard's top pediatric brain cancer doctors to come and provide guidance and assistance in program development.

We are committed to Nebraska. We are committed to Omaha. One of my life's works will be to assist in the creation of this tertiary center for pediatric brain cancer treatment. It has been one of the most challenging things I've ever had to participate in. Institutional politics is a grind. As a self-employed entrepreneur, I sometimes wish I could just point and click to make decisions and things happen. It is not that way when you are dealing with the state legislature, a board of regents, the board of directors for a children's hospital, and all of the various doctors with various administrative positions.

All we want to do is help kids.

If you ever find yourself in a situation—and you know that your intentions are pure and good, not for selfish reasons…keep pushing. Do not listen to the crowd. Do not find the quit button. Instead, find the button that says IDGAF and smash it.

In retrospect, I firmly believe that it was part of God's plan for us go through such a miserable experience in Omaha. Given that experience and our later exposures to some of the best care in the world, we became well suited to advocate for change. And even though the program in Nebraska is slowly trudging, we have at least shined a light on an under-served area and important need.

My wife and I have fully forgiven the facility that gave my son a fully conscious spinal tap. That refused to speak to us. That misdiagnosed my son and cost us nearly thirty days at a hospital treating a disease that he did not have. That accused my son of having "hospitalitis" instead of seizures. That operated on my son and nearly slit his cerebral artery.

Regardless of all of that, it is God's plan that forgiveness be complete and enthusiastic. The reason is simple—we must help kids. The bottom line is that Nebraska kids deserve a treatment close to home. One more time: we do it for the kids. I do not care whom I offend. Omaha must get better at treating this disease.

I am hopeful that someday soon we will have a fully functioning center of excellence. While there are a few components that are starting to improve, there is still a lot of work to be done. We advocate. Help fundraise. And encourage.

I am a stubborn Nebraskan. Our family will not stop until kids in Nebraska can drive to Omaha and get the same level of treatment had they continued on to Eppley and jumped on an airplane to Boston. Nebraska families cannot afford that kind of disruption in their lives. Some cannot even afford the plane ticket. Literally.

Chapter Twenty-Six

THE REX EFFECT

Rex Burkhead is not just consistent on the football field. This running back from Plano, Texas, has averaged over four yards per carry his entire football career (which has spanned from junior high to the New England Patriots). He is a sturdy football player you can trust.

But Rex's output on the football field pales in comparison to his output as a friend, family supporter, and advocate for child brain cancer. In early 2011, when Rex first put on a wristband, he made a commitment to Jack and our family. He was going to be there for us until the end. That same commitment still stands today. Since that first meeting, his love, support, and encouragement have been unwavering. The bright spot in Jack's difficult journey has been his relationship with Rex.

I have always told people, "You don't just wake up one day and decide that you want to be friends with Rex Burkhead. Rather, Rex gets to choose who he wants to be friends with." Remarkably, he has chosen Jack and our family.

During Rex's junior football campaign at Nebraska, our family traveled to the Capital One Citrus Bowl in Orlando, Florida. Two nights before the game, we had the opportunity to go out for supper with Rex and his parents.

We met them in the lobby. We were then escorted to a full-size player bus, which took us to the NBA restaurant—a place Rex had requested. Rex played arcade games with Jack before supper. It was an early sampling of what was yet to come: Rex putting himself before others. Always.

When he was drafted by the Bengals, we were able to make it to Cincinnati for a game in 2015. We also were able to see Rex play for the Bengals in Kansas City during a preseason game. It was difficult getting to Cincinnati, especially with all of the media trips and medical appointments still going on. However, we did the best that we could.

One of the earliest things our family did was change our television package from Dish Network to DIRECTV so we could get the NFL Sunday Ticket. That allowed us to watch every single NFL game that Rex played in.

After Rex was drafted by the Bengals, Geoff Hobson, a writer for the Bengals, reached out to our family to write a story about the NFL rookie. I expressed to him that Rex was going to be a major asset for the Bengals if they used him the right way. I think Geoff thought that I was joking. He was skeptical that Rex, a sixth-round draft pick, would even make the team. I assured him that Rex would be in the final fifty-two players and the Bengals were lucky to have him.

The Bengals did not use Rex like they should have. During Rex's last game, he had over one hundred yards rushing. It was a nice display of his talents heading into free agency. Marvin Lewis, head coach at the time, was a nice enough guy—just too shy about playing Rex more. In fact, soon after Rex was drafted, Marvin Lewis sent Jack a number 33 Bengals jersey. With it was a handwritten note mentioning that it was the first-ever Burkhead Bengals jersey.

It was like a dream come true for our family when Rex was traded from the Bengals to the New England Patriots. Since 2011, we had traveled to Boston several times a year for medical appointments. During this time, we became quite familiar with and fond of Boston's pro sports teams. The moods of medical doctors and nurses alike were influenced by how the professional teams were doing. A good game on Sunday meant good appointments on Monday. That was why, when we were in Boston, we always cheered for the home team. It became addictive. I suppose when someone moves to Nebraska, they may experience a similar phenomenon.

After Rex and his wife Danielle relocated to Boston, we saw them on their pro turf much more often. There were many occasions when we would either meet him for supper or he'd join us at Fenway Park for a Red Sox game.

I have countless memories of Rex treating my family as his family. An entire book could be devoted to his graciousness. Thus, when we would go and see Rex play, it was more than just a game. For Jack, it was like going to support a big brother. For me, it was like going to support a nephew—or a long-lost son.

Rex's football career became an extension of our entire family. This was just part of what we did.

As Jack was preparing for a Big Ten Network rewind about the run (which included an interview with Rex), I helped him organize his thoughts. I asked Jack, "What is your favorite memory since the run? Meeting the President? The ESPYs?"

He did not hesitate. It was a specific Patriots game experience that none of us would forget. It was the AFC Championship in Kansas City.

As the 2018 football season came to a close and the Patriots zeroed in on the playoffs, it became apparent they would play Kansas City in Kansas City in the AFC Championship. We jumped on getting tickets—it was too close not to go. Jack and his best friend, his cousin Hudson, traveled with my brother and me to Kansas City for the game. Boy, was it cold. At kickoff, it was ten degrees. With the wind chill, it was below.

Whenever Jack and I travel together, it always comes with about a ten-minute in-service on his medications. At the time, Jack was taking twenty-two pills a day. He was on cancer therapy medications (the clinical trial drugs) and multiple epilepsy medications to prevent seizures. We also carried an emergency anti-seizure medication known as Clonazepam in case he had a seizure that wouldn't go away. It was with me at all times, as it had been on countless hunting and fishing trips before.

I mentioned it was cold. The game was miserably cold. It was so cold that it was hard to watch. During the first half, I had been in communication with Rick Burkhead. We were going to make our way toward his seats at halftime, just to say hello and warm up. Halftime arrived; we grabbed a hot dog and began trekking across Arrowhead—and Jack started having a seizure. As I mentioned, a typical seizure for Jack at this point in time involved him becoming confused and unable to respond for one to two minutes. After about five minutes of the seizure, he wasn't snapping out of it. With each minute, it grew worse and worse. The concern was it would become grand mal...which can be nearly akin to a stroke. It was at times like this (which were not often, thank God) that we would administer the Clonazepam. One problem: I'd forgotten the medication in the car...nearly one mile away from the stadium.

Up to that point, Jack had only experienced two grand mal seizures. Both were so violent that they nearly took his life. The first was in Atkinson at the onset of his initial diagnosis.

The second occurred in January of 2016, just two years prior. When Jack and Mom were coming home from Boston, they were sitting on a tarmac in Atlanta on a DELTA flight for Omaha. As the airplane left the gate, it happened. Jack began staring off into space and would not come out of it. Moments later, he started convulsing and seizing. A cardiologist on the plane ran over and prepared to administer CPR. The flight attendants scrambled for the bag. A few minutes later, Jack was inside an ambulance heading to an Atlanta hospital.

Suffice it to say, our experiences with grand mal seizures were not pleasant.

In that freezing stadium, Jack's continuous complex partial seizure would not stop. I decided by the end of halftime that we needed to leave. I called Rick and told him we had to get Jack out of there. Rick volunteered to come with me and help. He was worried about Jack. I assured him we were good and wished him luck in the second half. After convincing my brother Mike and Hudson to stay at the game, Jack and I started heading towards the exit.

I was panicked. If we did not get to the car soon, it would escalate into a full grand mal—and probably another ambulance ride. After about five to seven minutes of searching for an exit, a kind stadium usher, who was also a schoolteacher, helped escort us to the gate. As we walked, he mentioned that there was no re-admittance into the stadium. At that point, I was resigned to the fact that returning to the game was a fantasy.

Before we fully exited, the kind usher explained to the front gate personnel that my son was having a seizure, we were going to go take some pills, and we would be back. The usher yelled at us as we left, "Be sure to come back to this gate."

Jack had reached status epilepticus—a continuous seizure state. I had to drag him; it was almost time to carry him.

We'd parked nearly a mile away. Thankfully, we were able to flag down a person driving a golf cart. We hopped on and they took us to the car. Once at our vehicle, I warmed my son up and got the meds in him.

I immediately contacted Bri. She could tell I was panicked. Jack had not had a seizure like this in a long time. In fact, I'd never actually seen one like this. I was trying to figure out if it was time to find a hospital in Kansas City.

The medication started kicking in. Jack came back to me a bit. Then, he looked at me and said, "Dad, I want to go back to the game." Still on the phone with Bri, I relayed how Jack was doing and that he wanted to go back into the game.

I was completely blown away by what I was seeing and hearing. I was doing worse than he was. I was still completely gripped in terror and adrenaline.

Mom and I conferred some more. With Jack practically begging at this point, we decided to go back to the game. I could not believe how effective the emergency seizure medications were.

Nine minutes remained in the fourth quarter when we got back to our seats. It was getting good. The Patriots needed to drive the ball and score a touchdown to put the game into overtime.

With the Patriots near the goal line and time running out, Tom Brady handed the football to Rex. Rapture immediately overcame us.

Rex plunged in for a touchdown from two yards out. We went berserk.

In the midst of overtime, the Patriots again found themselves on the Kansas City goal line, desperately needing to score—this time, to win the game. Only a few minutes after Rex's tying touchdown, Brady handed the ball to him again.

My chest exploded and tears covered my cheeks as I witnessed Rex score another touchdown. This touchdown punched his ticket to the Super Bowl.

That was a defining day of overcoming for people I love deeply. Jack overcame eight years of battling a brain tumor to get to that moment. He wouldn't let that tumor keep him from the experience of a lifetime. His staring down that seizure during halftime continues to inspire me.

For Rex, he'd spent seven weeks of that season on the bench due to injury. Rex was a true warrior and inspiration.

Mike, Hudson, Jack, and I all stared at each other. What had just happened?

We met Rex and his family outside the stadium after the game. I was beyond emotional. I could not talk without choking up. I felt overwhelmed by God's graciousness. I wrapped Rex in a giant hug and told him how proud we all were. We told Rex about how we'd almost missed his moment of glory, and he instantly asked how he could help. Rex being Rex…selfless in even his most profound moment of his historic football career.

It was Jack's favorite memory for many beautiful and deserving reasons.

When I was buying tickets to that AFC Championship, I made a deal with my wife. I told her that we would go to this game in lieu of going to the Super Bowl.

That was a mistake. I should never have said that.

While I meant what I'd said to Bri at the time, I was unbelievably overcome with what we'd experienced at Arrowhead that day; I went back to the hotel and shopped Super Bowl tickets until three in the morning with Mike. The next day, we slept in. We got back in barely enough time to avoid angering our spouses. By Thursday, I had secured Super Bowl tickets. Jack and I were going to the Super Bowl in Atlanta.

In February of 2019, Jack and I attended Super Bowl LIII—just the two of us. We'd naturally wanted to take the entire family, as was tradition. However, each ticket's price made that impossible. So, I went with my son. It was a fantastic trip.

The day before the game, we attended the NFL Experience. This was a carnival-like event hosted by the NFL. While walking through the exhibits, I noted a line comprised of a lot of fathers and sons. They were waiting to try and kick a field goal. As I watched, I noted that Tate Donovan was in line. I subtly pointed to Tate and reminded Jack that it was Tate who'd handed him his ESPY back in 2013. Jack's eyes brightened in recognition.

We walked over to Tate. "Mr. Donovan," I said politely.

He acknowledged and gave a slight smile and head nod.

"Do you remember giving an ESPY to a little boy from Nebraska in 2013?" I asked.

"Absolutely—how could I forget?" Mr. Donovan asked.

The warmth of rekindling that ESPYs night held the air. A pleasant discussion ensued. Tate asked about how Jack was doing and what the prognosis was. He is a good person.

It was certainly wonderful meeting him there. I often think that "chance meetings" like that are not chance at all, but instead carefully placed and organized by the Man upstairs.

The night before the Super Bowl, we saw that the New York Post published a story about Rex and his relationship with Jack. The story highlighted Rex's heroic performance in Kansas City and Jack's return to the game after battling a seizure at halftime. My mind surged straight back into that moment in Arrowhead Stadium; it felt completely fresh again. The story filled me with gratitude for Rex and thankfulness to the Good Lord for my son and for our being in Atlanta that day.

Before the game, we attended a Super Bowl tailgate party hosted by ESPN. It was fantastic to see Rex's family before the big moment. We then left the tailgate party with them and walked to the game together. They were so kind to include us in some of their Super Bowl festivities.

The Super Bowl game was nothing short of awesome. There we sat, in the Atlanta Mercedes-Benz Stadium, watching our own Rex Burkhead in the Super Bowl. It was a dream come true on so many levels. Not only were we excited for Rex and his family, but I was thrilled to have been able to take my son to a Super Bowl. It was my first Super Bowl as well. It was so fulfilling to have that experience with my son.

During the game, I texted a few pics to Bo Pelini. After all, we had him to thank for Jack's meeting Rex Burkhead.

Once again, Rex had the game-clinching run. Late in the fourth quarter, with time running out, Rex rattled off a twenty-seven-yard run, giving the Patriots a fresh set of downs to run out the clock. It was unbelievable. We vibrated.

There is something very special about the Super Bowl. It's not just a game. A lot of people have told me, "You should go to the Super Bowl sometime."

They are right. You should.

As luck would have it, Jack's clinical trial required us to be in Boston fall of 2019. With some very minor manipulation on my part, we were able to schedule it around the Patriots' season opener against the Steelers. It was a Sunday night game, and the atmosphere was Super Bowl-esque, in its own right. And this time, the entire family attended.

After the game, Rex took our family underneath the stadium and we joined his teammates and their families for a postgame meal. We then stepped out onto the field and soaked it all in.

On the drive back to our hotel in Boston, we listened to some of the Patriot's postgame coverage. They were raving about Rex

Burkhead. Between the chunks of conversation, commercials played about a fundraiser that Rex was involved in for the Team Jack Foundation: Credit Union Kids at Heart.

With so many amazing things happening around us, we could only revel in how grateful we were that our son had Rex Burkhead in his life.

Chapter Twenty-Seven

FOOTBALL'S CONSTANT PRESENCE

In the summer of 2019, Bri and I toiled over whether or not we would let Jack play junior high football. The year before, Jack's seventh-grade year, football had been off the table due to breaking his leg.

To help us reach our decision, Bri and I consulted with Jack's neuro-oncologist, neurosurgeon, and neurologist from Boston. Unsurprisingly, brain cancer doctors do not want children who've undergone multiple brain tumor surgeries to play football. Regardless, they ultimately said that the decision was in our hands. After weighing all of the risks…Jack would be playing football.

In July of 2019, approximately one week before football practice began, Jack purchased a pair of Nike Shark football cleats. I recommended the Nike Sharks, as those were what I wore when I played high school football. I'll never forget perusing the store aisles stacked with gear; it was awesome. I knew to enjoy the little things.

Jack's first organized football game occurred soon after Labor Day. It was in Ainsworth, Nebraska. It was a standard middle school football game between two eight-man schools. It was kind of sloppy for a first game, but a hell of a lot of fun to watch. Jack had his grandparents, parents, and sisters all there. We watched, tearfully, as Jack played his favorite sport. He started at center. He played some downs on defense. He seemed to do well and had a noticeably hot engine. From all appearances, I told myself, I think we may have a football player here.

At the end of the game, I insisted on a photo with my son. I needed to capture this "proud father" moment, after all we had been through. About three hours later, from the comfort of our own kitchen, I went to send out a Tweet to thank God for answered prayers. I showed the Tweet to my wife before pressing the send button. I went to bed.

The next morning, I noted the Tweet had gone viral and was now being talked about on local media. A day or two later, I received a phone call from *The Washington Post*; they wanted to run a story about Jack. I was also contacted by the Associated Press.

On Friday of that week, a producer from *ABC World News Tonight* contacted me at my office. This was at 2:00 p.m. She stated that David Muir wanted to feature Jack on the *ABC Evening News*. We scrambled to get her video clips and photos from Monday's game. As it turned out, *ABC World News Tonight* didn't just have some small story in mind. Jack was their Person of the Week.

During my discussion with the ABC producer, I put her through the drill we'd developed six years prior. Like all other prior media appearances, I required her to assure us that ABC would talk about the foundation and the need for child brain cancer research funding. Thankfully, she agreed. During that "Person of the Week" telecast, David Muir talked about the Team Jack Foundation, they showed a clip of the website, and they told people where to go if they wanted to join the fight against child brain cancer. Score for kids with brain tumors. This was a great opportunity to raise awareness. Again, we were doing perfectly fine before this came along. However, we saw this as an opportunity to once again scream our mantra on national television.

As the football season of 2019 rolled along, we were deep into following Jack's games and Huskers football. We were having a great time. Then, on some Wednesday afternoon, I was contacted by an ESPN producer. He wanted to see if Jack and I would appear on ESPN's *College GameDay*, as they were going to be in Lincoln next Saturday to cover the Nebraska-Ohio State game.

After consultation with Bri (naturally), I called back to confirm our attendance. And they also obliged to our conditions. So, when Maria Taylor was interviewing us on *College GameDay*, she gave us an open mic to talk about the foundation and the need for research funding. She was amazing.

Due to our boldness in these television interviews, we continued to keep the Team Jack Foundation relevant. But more importantly, we were able to raise critical awareness for pediatric brain cancer. These opportunities were nothing short of a free TV commercial for our brain cancer foundation.

If you ever find yourself desperately desiring to send a message, be courageous. If you are going to put yourself out there, do it for the right reasons. It can be very difficult to not get caught up in all of it. For me, by keeping our goal in the forefront, I've grown indifferent to the idea of appearing on television. TV does not need Jack, me, or my family. But TV does need to broadcast, as much as possible, that pediatric brain cancer is the leading childhood cancer cause of death. If you're going to put me on it, that's the message you will hear.

The fall of 2019 brought an unusual surprise for Jack. Sitting at my office desk, I received a text message from Coach Jeff Jamrog, the same man who'd set up Jack's touchdown run. He was now at Midland University in Fremont, Nebraska, as the head football coach. Coach Jamrog asked me to give him a call sometime. I called him right away.

He started asking me what kind of student Jack was and if he had plans to go to college. I told him that he was pretty much a straight-A student, and we planned on him attending.

"Andy," Coach said warmly, "I'm calling on behalf of Midland University, because we want to offer Jack a full-ride football scholarship."

"…Are you serious?" I asked.

"Jack embodies the type of student athlete that we want at Midland, and I think he would be a great fit. I don't care if he plays a down of football in high school—he is somebody we want in the program."

Coach and I then made arrangements for Jack to visit the school in late October. I informed Coach that we would not tell Jack about this amazing offer, as it wasn't our news to tell. He was excited about that.

When we arrived for the tour, Midland rolled out the red carpet for Jack. The experience felt like a genuine recruitment trip. There was a conference in front of the entire team with the media. Coach talked about his prior experience with Jack and explained what Midland was offering. That was the first time Jack had heard the news. His facial expression was unforgettable.

My son stared at me and whispered, "Is he serious, Dad?"

"Yes, he is serious," I beamed. "Congratulations, Jack."

The thing that really got me—as his father—was how incredibly real the whole thing felt. Here was Jack, who'd played a whopping five junior high football games, being recruited like he was a five-star athlete with four years of high school football under his belt. Coach made the entire experience so special and unique for all of us.

"Jack, I know you are going to have a lot of colleges come after you, but I can tell you this…" Coach commented to my son, "No one is going to recruit you harder than Midland University."

Following the team gathering, Coach Jamrog spent another hour with our family to show us around campus. At one point, Jack asked about the food at college. Coach Jamrog was excited to show him the cafeteria. It passed Jack's inspection.

Bri and I do not know what the future holds for Jack. He is a very normal freshman in high school. He is going to try and play high school athletics. Of course, he loves football. He also enjoys basketball and track. His seizure disability and future treatments will unfortunately hold some sway, as a third surgery is currently being discussed. The timing of this surgery, if it occurs, could be a game-changer for his athletic career.

For now, we continue reminding ourselves that today is all that any of us are promised…and we will let tomorrow worry about itself. So, with that in mind, he is lifting weights, working hard, and going to try and find his way onto the gridiron this fall.

After all, he has a football scholarship to fulfill.

Chapter Twenty-Eight
ATTITUDE OF GRATITUDE

Our family and the Team Jack Foundation have tried to have an attitude of gratitude every step of the way. We are not remarkable people. The Team Jack movement is remarkable due to where we live. Nebraskans made what we have accomplished possible.

Another amazing thing about the Team Jack movement is that if a single one of four particular people had not been involved in Jack's life very early on, the movement may have ceased to exist. Those people were Rex Burkhead, Bo Pelini, Keith Zimmer, and Randy York.

Rex's relationship with Jack paved the way by wearing that wristband during his junior and senior years at Nebraska. He ignited our movement. He is now a charter member of the foundation and its biggest supporter.

Keith Zimmer's involvement was amazing. Keith was the person who set up the meeting between Jack and Rex back on September 15th, 2011. Without that meeting, this book would not exist, and the experiences described herein would've never occurred. But Keith's support has gone well beyond just scheduling a meeting. He has worked with the football program in creating and hosting an annual road race event. This event has raised nearly three hundred thousand dollars for child brain cancer research, and the dollars raised at this event now go to the Team Jack project in Omaha.

Deservedly so, Keith was the first Team Jack Foundation MVP of the Year Award winner.

Then there is Randy York. Randy is the ultimate Huskers insider. Randy is a prolific sportswriter; he worked for Huskers.com during Jack's first visit with Rex. He wrote a story about that visit. That story then caught the eye of ABC television, and the ball was rolling. He then later went on to write numerous Team Jack Foundation stories and blog articles. These articles, undoubtedly, help raise awareness and solidify the brand all across the state of Nebraska. With this brand awareness and association with Huskers football, countless dollars were raised. Randy is very special to our family and our cause.

The final leg on this four-legged chair is Bo Pelini. Bo catapulted the Team Jack Foundation beyond our wildest imaginations by having the guts to put a seven-year-old in a football game. Bo is one of the greatest heroes in this entire movement. While some Nebraskans may not care for Bo, this Nebraskan will be forever grateful for all that he did for my son and the pediatric brain cancer cause. At Rex's senior football banquet in December of 2012, Bo specifically sought out Jack and me.

After finding us, he told us not to be strangers. "Andy, I know Rex is going to be gone and all that, but don't stop coming around. Jack is a part of this team, and he will be for as long as I'm around."

When Bo Pelini says something, he means it. To this day, Bo continues to support Team Jack. Each year, he sponsors pediatric brain cancer kids at the Team Jack Gala. He silently but powerfully continues to plug.

In the spring of 2020, when asked about the foundation, Bo's support for the cause remained unwavering: "I will support the Team Jack Foundation until the day that I die."

I am so grateful for all he has done.

If any of these legs were removed from this chair, we would no longer have a chair at all.

While there are countless other supporters that are involved with Team Jack today, these were some of the original core. I am honored to have spoken of them in this book.

While these amazing experiences all happened to our family—and our son, specifically—we do not believe that it was necessarily an accident. For some reason, God chose to give Jack a brain tumor. For some reason, God chose Jack to score a touchdown. For some reason, God gave Jack these incredible opportunities. Everything has been a gift. We have always felt and believed that it was incumbent upon us to do as much as possible with these incredible blessings. We wanted to make this a blessing for the cure, not just for Jack and our family.

We have tried to be selfless through these experiences. We have tried to maintain our integrity and Nebraskan humility. There have been times where my ego has flared up—but thankfully, I am blessed with a wife like Bri. She is a beautiful old soul. To have a spouse with an old soul is truly a blessing of the deepest kind.

It can sometimes be difficult when the media is swirling around you, when your Facebook posts are getting thousands of likes, and when your Tweets are going viral. It is sometimes tempting to incessantly look at your phone to see what the next person said. Thankfully, due to our faith and Christ-centered life-approach, we have not become intoxicated by these events. What is more, I'm glad that we live in Atkinson—because Jack is actually a bigger celebrity in Lincoln and Omaha. In Atkinson, he is just another ornery high school kid. Yes, I said it…high school kid.

Praise the Lord!

If there's only one thing I want you to take away from our journey and this book, it is this:

If God opens the door, run through it.

Chapter Twenty-Nine

ENCORE:
SPEAKING THE TRUTH
IN LOVE TO PARENTS

Our family has been in and out of brain tumor treatment for nearly ten years. These experiences have taught us some valuable lessons. Here, I shall devote a chapter to sharing some of those lessons.

This chapter was specifically written for parents who may have just received the news that their child has a brain tumor. It is intended to educate, support, and inspire you—all at the same time.

Learning that your child has a brain tumor is one of the most devastating things you could ever hear in your life. The news knocks the wind out of you. Literally. Life transitions immediately from worrying about work, soccer schedules, and what's for supper, to wondering where the hell you go next. While the steps getting to this diagnosis were likely painful for your family, it does not compare to the pain of the diagnosis itself. News of a brain tumor diagnosis is debilitating. You become focused on savoring every moment with your sick child—while simultaneously trying to spare a few moments for your healthy children.

At this point in life, you are resigned to the fact that whichever medical professionals were around you during the diagnosis process will be the ones fighting the brain tumor. Your energy to research other options is not there. You do not have the strength or desire to research what it means for your child to have a brain tumor. You haven't the drive to find out who is widely considered the best in your area for pediatric brain tumor treatment. Your internal power is at an all time low in every category—except hugging and loving your child.

The steps you take after learning that your child has a brain tumor are critical. You must fight through the diagnosis-induced debilitation and educate yourself on what your options are.

Brain Tumor Basics

First things first. You must realize that your child has an extraordinarily rare disease. Depending on who your family doctor or pediatrician is, your child may be the first patient they've ever had with a brain tumor. Some brain tumors grow fast. Others grow slower. The speed of growth determines their grade. Tumors are graded based upon the World Health Organization's (WHO) grading scale. According to the National Cancer Institute at the National Institutes of Health, brain tumors are graded as follows (information from NCI):

A. Grade I: The cells look nearly like normal brain cells, and they grow slowly.
B. Grade II: The tissue is malignant. The cells look less normal than Grade I.
C. Grade III: The malignant tissue has cells that look very different from normal cells.
D. Grade IV: The malignant tissue has cells that look completely abnormal and tend to grow quickly.

According to the NCI, Grade I tumors are low grade, Grade II tumors are intermediate grade, and Grade III and IV are high grade. They are all bad. I've seen kids with Grade IV tumors survive many years. I have watched low grade tumors kill, blind, and cripple children. There is no such thing as a "good" brain tumor. They all suck and all deserve equal research attention.

The Treatment Process

Medicine is not an exact science. Various medical institutes in this country take varying approaches to how brain tumors are treated. For that reason, it is not uncommon for parents to get multiple opinions on their child's diagnosis. The doctors who should (oftentimes) be involved in your child's care are highly sub-specialized, pediatric-based medical practitioners. Generally speaking, the treatment process follows this chronology:

1. MRI. Magnetic resonance imaging (MRI) is step one. This type of imaging allows doctors to determine the size and location of the tumor. It also helps to plan any surgical or radiological intervention. Other imaging may also be used, which is not referenced here.

2. Pre-surgical Psychological Evaluation. The gold standard for pediatric brain tumor treatment insists that all children, prior to treatment for their brain tumor, undergo an intense diagnostic study so that a psychological baseline is established prior to any surgery or radiotherapy. Such a test will become a part of the clinical picture. Pretreatment testing can be compared to post-treatment testing to determine possible areas where therapeutic services may be needed. Such testing will also serve as a compass to keep things on course in the future. Future deviations from any post-treatment testing may signal a tumor re-occurrence. This is a valuable clinical piece. Parents should insist on this testing so that the child can reach their full potential as they grow up.

3. Surgery. There are two goals to surgical intervention. The foremost goal of surgery is to remove the brain tumor to the greatest extent possible. When a neurosurgeon attempts to remove a brain tumor, it is called a "resection." When a brain tumor is removed completely, it is called "gross total resection." A "near total resection" is when the tumor is almost entirely removed. A "subtotal resection" is when residual tumor remains to an extent greater than the near total resection standard. While a number of factors will affect the extent of resection, one of the key factors is the experience of the neurosurgeon. It is critical that an experienced pediatric neurosurgeon specializing in brain tumor removal performs your child's surgery. Many experienced oncological pediatric neurosurgeons have written and published medical journal articles about the importance of an experienced neurosurgeon conducting the surgery.

4. Pathological Study and Diagnosis. Following surgery, any tumor specimen removed during the surgical process will be sent to a laboratory to be studied by a pathologist. A pathologist is a medical doctor who specializes in examining tissue. Pathologists are doctors that have completed a four-year undergraduate program, four years of medical school, and three to four years of post graduate training in the form of a pathology residency. And it is unlikely that you will ever meet the pathologist that actually examines your child's brain tumor. Nonetheless, this physician is one of the most important in the process, and it is essential that you understand their role. While pathology is a specialty all to its own, a sub-specialty of this specialization is neuropathology. A neuropathologist is a doctor who focuses on examining brain tumors. Taking it further, a sub sub-specialty of this important area is a pediatric neuropathologist. Ideally, a child's brain tumor specimen is studied by this level of expert.

A pathologist, ultimately, will determine what grade your child's tumor is. They will also identify the type of tumor (e.g., pilocytic astrocytoma, medulloblastoma). Good pathology, however, does not stop there. The grade and tumor type should just be the beginning. Modern science now allows pathological study at the genetic level to identify any specific genetic mutations or abnormalities making a brain tumor grow. The identification of these mutations or abnormalities is critical as they will help dictate your child's eligibility to any clinical trials. Insist on genetic testing of your child's tumor. If you are at a facility that cannot perform this function, a second opinion should be obtained.

5. Chemotherapy. Depending on the extent of resection, type of tumor, grade, genetic mutations, and a host of other factors, your child may or may not need chemotherapy. Essentially, the pathological diagnosis will help your child's oncologist determine which direction to go regarding whether or not chemotherapy is needed.

6. Radiation. Again, depending on the tumor's extent of resection, type, grade, and location, your child may or may not need radiation therapy. It is important to note that there are various medical opinions in existence regarding when and how frequently radiation therapy should be used. Radiation therapy presents one of the biggest concerns in this area of medicine as a young child's brain is still developing—and radiation is tied to serious morbidities in terms of adverse development in children. Sometimes, however, it is necessary for the survival of the child. In such cases, developmental concerns are subservient thoughts. Notably, new developments in radiation therapy—particularly proton beam therapy—allow more direct and targeted radiation, which can reduce the overall subjected field and decrease radiation impact on non-tumor areas. In addition to developmental concerns, radiation has also been linked to causing long-term adverse effects (secondary tumors, accelerating lower-grade tumors to higher grades, etc.).

Your Child's Brain Tumor Treatment

If your child has a brain tumor, it is important to assemble a dream team of medical professionals. Your child deserves this. Due to pediatric brain tumors being so rare, doctors that are at the highest level of treatment generally treat only brain tumors. While it is important to have experienced doctors, even more important is that your doctors communicate as a team. Good pediatric brain tumor care starts with a team of doctors who work together on your child's case.

Your child's dream team should include the following:

- Pediatric Neurologist (preferably Onco Neurologist)
- Pediatric Neurosurgeon (preferably Onco Neurosurgeon)
- Pediatric Neuro Oncologist
- Pediatric Neuropathologist
- Pediatric Neuro-Radiologist
- Pediatric Neuropsychologist

And, if necessary:

- Pediatric Endocrinologist
- Pediatric Ophthalmologist

A Good Place to Start

There's a good chance that you are currently at a medical facility that does not offer the team of sub-specialists as outlined previously. At the minimum, a good place to start is with the world renowned Pediatric Brain Tumor Consortium. This is a professional association of the leading pediatric brain tumor treatment institutions in America. It is possible that your hospitalist, general family doctor, or pediatrician hasn't even heard of this association. However, a second opinion from one of these institutions will put your child in the best position possible to defeat this disease.

Very Important: What You Absolutely Need to Know

Not all NFL quarterbacks are created equally. Given the choice, would you rather have Tom Brady leading your team—or the guy from the team that finished under .500 last year? If your child has a brain tumor, you need a good quarterback. Oftentimes, the quarterback of your child's care team is the neurosurgeon. Now remember: their experience and specialization are extremely important considerations.

An experienced neurosurgeon can be the difference between needing just one or two whole surgeries. They can be the difference between continuous seizures or never seizing again. And, in some cases, they can be the difference between life or death. As corroboration, we note with great particularity that expert pediatric neurosurgeons specializing in brain tumor care have even gone so far as to say that there is "acceptable morbidity" to consider going in a second time. That is, if your child had an unsuccessful surgery the first time, you should consider having a more experienced neurosurgeon operate a second time—despite the risks associated with that surgery. It has been statistically proven that such second surgeries performed by industry leaders in pediatric brain tumor removals "achieve a high incidence of GTR (gross total resection) or NTR (near total resection)." Pediatric neurosurgeons performing at the highest societal level give quite clear advice: "We suggest that referral to a pediatric neurosurgeon experienced in brain tumor surgery should be considered for pediatric patients with residual tumor after initial resection."

To maximize your child's opportunity and reduce the likelihood of a second surgery, we would recommend that you consult with a highly skilled and experienced pediatric neurosurgeon as soon as possible post-diagnosis. While there are certainly other options available, the Pediatric Brain Tumor Consortium institutions will likely be the best route to finding the proper expertise to save your child's life.

An experienced neurosurgeon will not only be more comfortable with the deep anatomical parts of your child's brain, but (given their experience) they are better at being able to determine normal tissue from abnormal tissue. When a brain tumor is removed, it is done so under a microscope. The neurosurgeon looks at the brain tissue under the microscope. The more brain tumors a neurosurgeon has seen, the easier it is for them to recognize abnormal tissue from normal tissue. This experience is not only a matter of life or death, it can also dictate how much tumor is actually removed and how much healthy tissue is left behind.

In addition to a good pediatric neurosurgeon, one of the other leaders in your child's care should be a pediatric neuro oncologist. A pediatric neuro oncologist is an oncologist that specializes in child brain cancer. These professionals know the most about existing clinical trials, best practices in chemotherapy treatments, and current information about surgery and radiology. You will likely need to work with a Pediatric Brain Tumor Consortium facility to receive the benefit of a pediatric neuro oncologist. According to sources, there are fewer than forty pediatric neuro oncologists in the United States—which clearly highlights the extreme rarity of child brain tumors.

Seek Second Opinions

All aspects of pediatric brain tumor care involve a human being giving their subjective thought and opinion. Pathological diagnosis involves a human being looking under a microscope and counting the splitting cells. Radiologists, when looking at an MRI, are asked to identify and diagnose a tumor based upon their visual observation. A neurosurgeon's decision to remove more or less of a tumor is based upon their own personal observation.

In the end, due to the fact that so much human subjectivity is involved in pediatric brain tumor care, second and third opinions are essential to fighting the good fight. Dr. Jerome Goopman, a Harvard-based oncologist and the Dina and Raphael Recanati Chair of Medicine at Harvard Medical School, discusses the impossibility of complete uniformity in areas like radiology, simply because it deals with mere mortals—human beings. Experience in the specific area of pediatric brain tumors is the most important factor. If your doctor practices in areas other than pediatric brain tumors, then you are not likely dealing with the level of expertise that your child needs. When an NFL football team hires a quarterback, they do not want one that also plays baseball and basketball.

Technology Matters

Depending on where you are considering treatment, they may or may not have the most current technological resources available. By way of example, in 2006, Boston Children's Hospital's pediatric oncological neurosurgeon Liliana Goumnerova became the first neurosurgeon in North America to perform a brain tumor surgery using an intraoperative MRI operating room. This allowed the brain tumor patient to receive an MRI during the surgical procedure so the doctors could evaluate, as they went, whether they needed to remove more tumor or not—and how to do so safely. This surgical technology has been proven to increase brain tumor resection efficacy. Despite its proven advantages by researchers, there are still a great number of children's hospitals that do not have this technology.

Technology can also be a game-changer in pathology. While a good pediatric neuropathologist is important, so is their ability to conduct molecular study at the genetic level. Not all pathology labs in North America will be able to identify the exact genetic mutations or abnormalities that your child's brain tumor has. For that reason, a good question to ask your team is whether or not they will conduct genetic testing of your child's brain tumor.

AFTERWORD

Twice the Fight

By Michael Nicloy

I will always remember that Monday morning. I had just dropped off my kids at the sitter. It was a few minutes before 9 a.m., and my cell phone caller ID showed my friend, Andy Hoffman, was calling.

Andy and I had made our acquaintance about two months prior, to talk about publishing this very book. He had contacted me because he had a copy of a book I had published for another childhood cancer warrior, Dick Vitale. After "The Run" and the ESPY, Jack was honored at one of Dickie V's annual V Foundation Galas, and the Vitales and the Hoffmans have kept in contact to keep up on Jack and his cancer fight.

Andy and I became friends almost instantly during that call, as I am sure happens with everyone Andy meets. He has that way about him…with his passion for his family and the cause of raising money for pediatric brain cancer research, as well as his straightforward nature and Midwestern humility, it is impossible not to be a friend of this man. Sure, our friendship began as a business dealing, but once our business was settled, contract in place, we would talk like two guys who were friends, getting to know each other. We would talk about our families and kids, how Jack was doing, what our plans were for sending our kids to school in the fall, if there would be a college football season in this time of Covid-19, the Team Jack Foundation, his law practice, our mutual disdain and outright hatred of cancer. We talked about my kidney transplant and how I was doing, and how my living donor was doing eight years on. He cared, genuinely, about my condition, as much as I cared about Jack's and the foundation named for him which helps kids like Jack, and families like the Hoffmans. We talked about my publishing business. He gave me advice. I always enjoyed our conversations.

I met Bri on one of our many Zoom calls, and later I met Kylie Dockter, director of the foundation. In that short time, I felt welcomed by the Hoffman family, and the Team Jack Family. I introduced Andy to the editor of this book, RaeAnne Scargall, and after our meeting, we all stayed on the Zoom call and chatted about life in our respective areas of the country; RaeAnne in Tennessee, Andy in Nebraska, and me in Wisconsin.

That Monday morning, Andy did not sound like himself. His voice was weak and shaky, and I could tell right away something was wrong. I immediately thought something happened to Jack, but before I could ask what was wrong, Andy slowly told me that he had a seizure while jogging the day before, and had woken up in the emergency room. Later that day he had a biopsy. The news was not good…he was diagnosed with a brain tumor; glioblastoma!

"It's bad," he said. It was so sudden, but so advanced. Andy has done enough research, in his time, to know what he was facing. The Andy Hoffman I know is an extremely positive person; I could not find that in his voice that morning. The news was a shock, and he was struggling to speak, not just emotionally, but due to the tumor's effect on his brain. He was scared, and he was sad. He was devastated at the thought of his future and that of his wife and children.

I stumbled around trying to be encouraging and empathetic… *It's going to be alright, man! You're at the Mayo Clinic! That's the best place you can be right now! Those docs there are the best!*

I wasn't helpful. I was mourning my friend. I was sick about it. I felt terrible for him and the family. I was at a loss. How do you comfort someone who has spent all of these years living with the sadness and horror of a child with a brain tumor, and then, once that child is showing improvement—even showing signs of beating this heinous enemy—gets the absolute gut-punch of hearing that now he has it too?

Andy and I talked for a bit longer, and we cried together. He was sad and angry, but determined. He was staring down death, and the prospect of his children losing their dad, and his wife losing her husband. And that, to Andy Hoffman, was unacceptable.

Even though he was discouraged at his diagnosis, he knew nothing else but FIGHT. He didn't know anything else but using what strength he had to beat this tumor. It was a long shot, but there is no quit in Andy Hoffman—no quit on his life, and no quit on getting this book out as a way to raise awareness and dollars for childhood brain cancer research.

We spoke about the book before hanging up the phone. "Obviously, this changes things," he told me. "I gotta get this book done, before I…" he trailed off. He needed to see this project through to completion. He was, at the least, going to beat that tumor that way. We developed a plan to expedite the process of getting the book published, and Andy needed to work on a plan of a different kind: treatment for his tumor.

Getting Andy stabilized was the first challenge. He was declining rapidly. I spoke to him later that week, and the difference in just a few days was unsettling, and astounding. The tumor had grown significantly. The following week, he had at least two strokes, and once his six weeks of intense radiation began, he lost the ability to walk and had much more difficulty eating, speaking, and putting his thoughts together.

I had interviewed Andy's sister-in-law, Jacky, for this book, and I called her after Andy's diagnosis. I wanted to keep up on his treatment and progress. Jacky was great. Sending me texts every so often just to keep me posted. I am extremely grateful to her for that. Andy's treatment was tough. But Andy is tough, too.

In the last few weeks of his treatment, Andy was able to get back home to Atkinson for two different weekends. He regained his strength and was able to walk again. A friend helped him and Bri get a flight back home. The first weekend he went back, he was able to see Jack's first freshman football game. That was huge.

Andy and I talked briefly the following Monday, and I asked him about Jack's game. He replied simply, "It was awesome." What a gift it was for Andy to be able to witness that, to be with his family and his parents at home, if just for a short time. I was ecstatic for him. After all that went on with Jack's cancer, getting to the field for his first game was a major deal. For Andy to be able to witness that…it was, as Andy put it, awesome.

Jacky and I spoke on the phone a few times as well. I asked her about her thoughts on this new development.

She told me, "Andy being diagnosed with a brain tumor nine years after his son's diagnosis…it seems like…a really bad joke. They had the first episode with Jack, and it was tragic—like hitting rock bottom, thinking how am I going to get up and face this tomorrow, again? There were some tough times for them, and I can't even relate to how bad they were. But they picked up all the pieces and just powered forward, and they've powered forward ever since."

"I think of their daughter, Reese," Jacky continued, "she was four months old when Jack was diagnosed. This is all she knows: fighting brain tumors. She and her sister Ava have just grown up around it; it's just life for them. Part of me thinks it's not fair, going through it all for nine years…it's unbelievable to me that now they're doing it again. But I think, what's the story that comes out of this? There's no way that Andy is done. As soon as we heard about Andy, my husband said, 'Okay, we're going to switch from planning a funeral to fighting. What are we going to do? Because this is NOT the end.' There are miracles every day, and there is no way this is the end of the story. Stay tuned, there's a lot to happen. I believe that fully."

I asked Jacky about how Bri was doing. "Bri is a rock. She is strong for the kids, for me, for our family. I don't mean to simplify this too much, but she's done this before. She knows what to do, and she is going to do it again.

"I remember when Jack first started going through this, we would watch the girls, and Bri would ask us, 'How are you guys doing?'

"What? All that is going on with her son, and she still has the compassion to care about how the rest of us are. Honestly, she is very steady, very focused, and a very smart person. She's not too high, not too low; just steady. It amazes me, and here she is again, going through this fight, and once again, she is a rock. She is so supportive, and simply says, 'Okay, let's put on our fightin' boots and go on and tackle this.'"

The fight to beat pediatric brain cancer never ends. The mission of the Hoffmans and the Team Jack Foundation has always been to raise awareness and money for pediatric brain cancer research. After Andy's diagnosis, the Foundation launched a shirt to raise funds for the disease while supporting the Hoffmans new fight. It simply said, "Twice the Fight." The Foundation and the Hoffman family have used Andy's diagnosis as an opportunity to fulfill the mission of Team Jack. Shortly after that, Jacky and her family created the official book shirt with Andy's slogan, "If God opens a door, run through it!" which is exactly what they have done. With both shirts, one hundred percent of the proceeds benefit the Team Jack Foundation and their mission to fight child brain cancer.

While Rex Burkhead and I were working on his foreword for the book, we spoke about Andy's diagnosis…

Rex said, "Andy left me a voicemail telling me about his brain tumor. I was in shock at the news. I had to listen to his message again; this can't be real, I told myself. I just couldn't believe it. Everything this family has gone through and continues to go through with Jack, and now Andy…I really feel for them and just want to do everything I can to help. I had so many questions. What is next for them? How can I help? How is their situation with the kids at home?

"Andy and I are friends. Genuine friends. When we talked, it was a very emotional phone call. I just tried to let him know that we would be there; me, my family. Whatever they needed, we would be happy to help, and would be there beside him through his fight. Andy has so much strength, he knows about the disease as good as anybody, just from his son's fight continually."

Rex agrees with Jacky about Bri (and I would guess anyone who has ever met her), "Bri is an unbelievable woman—very strong and strong-willed, and does so much for the family from the mom standpoint. She is keeping the kids on their routine through all of the things going on with Jack, and now with Andy. But as a mother, she also worries about all the possibilities of what could happen in the future, and she keeps her family positive, and makes sure they're having fun. That's the type of person she is, and the kind of figure she is for that family. Andy knows that. During one of our calls after his diagnosis, he told me, 'I just got so lucky, having Bri. I don't know how she does it. I don't know how she puts up with all of this.'"

I don't think Bri views it that way. She doesn't "put up" with anything. This is life. Bri is a partner and mother who has a son and husband with brain cancer. In life, you do what you need to do. Yes, one has to be strong in such circumstances, and there is no question about Bri's strength.

The battle to end childhood brain cancer is grossly underfunded, and treatments for children with brain cancer are outdated. The Hoffman family's passion is to make research a priority through the Team Jack Foundation.

Andy wrote this book to document and share Jack's journey and shine a light on the disease itself. Little did he know as he was writing it that he would be diagnosed with a brain tumor. That will not stop Andy fighting for kids with brain cancer. The mission is stronger than ever.

Now, it is twice the fight.

ACKNOWLEDGMENTS

Andy & Bri Hoffman would like to acknowledge and thank the following for their continued support of the Team Jack Foundation and mission of funding childhood brain cancer research.

Kenneth & Verna Mae Jessen Trust
The Home Agency | Jim and Sharri Baldonado Family
Fat Brain Toys | Mark and Karen Carson Family
Farmers Mutual of Nebraska
Credit Union Kids at Heart
Robert and Kimberly Westerkamp Family
Rex and Danielle Burkhead Family
Rick and Robyn Burkhead Family
Richard and Patricia Galyen Family
Dan and Tami Campbell Family
Bo and Mary Pat Pelini Family
Mike and Deb Kelly Family
Dr. Kari and Dr. Jim Galyen Family
Pinnacle Bancorp, Inc. | Sid Dinsdale
Nathan Waggoner Memorial
The Atmos Energy/Robert W. Best Charitable Giving Fund
Midwest Oral & Maxillofacial Surgery PC
Monte Selden Trucking, Inc.
Team Jack Husker Alumni Chapter
DJ's Dugout Sports Bar

Green Plains, Inc.
Nebraska Football
University of Nebraska-Lincoln Life Skills Department | Keith Zimmer
University of Nebraska Medical Center
Children's Hospital & Medical Center at Omaha
Dana-Farber Cancer Institute
Boston Children's Hospital
The NASCAR Foundation
Mark Burch Motorsports
Applied Connective Technologies
Tim Pratt | Dietze Music
Brian Kreikemeier | B&B Video Productions
Travis Scott | RainierDigital
Randy York
Cody Thomas
Mike Flood
Marilyn Mecham
Hal, Julie, and Jeff Hanson
Nebraska Brain Tumor Families | Team Jack Family
Team Jack Board of Directors and Volunteers

ABOUT THE AUTHOR

Andrew Hoffman

Andrew Hoffman grew up on a farm three miles east of Spencer, Nebraska. He received his Bachelor of Political Science Degree with High Honors from South Dakota State University, and his law degree from the University of South Dakota School of Law and was a Sterling Honor Society Graduate.

Andrew is married to Brianna Hoffman, a Doctor of Pharmacy. Brianna is a hospital pharmacist and also served as the office manager for Andrew Hoffman Law. Andrew and Brianna also are actively involved in farming and ranching. Together, they have three kids—Jack, Ava, and Reese.

In July 2020, Andrew was diagnosed with a brain tumor causing his early retirement from the practice of law.

Previously, he was an active small-town attorney deep in the heart of Rural Nebraska. From representing farmers in real estate transactions, to planning a rancher's succession plan, Andrew enjoyed his robust agriculturally influenced law practice. Andrew practiced law with a deep sense of commitment and loyalty to his clients. As the son of rural farmers and entrepreneurs, Andrew feels a genuine connection to each and every one of his clients. He is passionate about helping people.

Giving back to his community is interwoven into Andrew's fabric. Hundreds of hours are spent each year, helping the communities he serves.

In addition to his local volunteer projects, Andrew has become well-known as a national advocate for research funding for childhood brain cancer—a disease which affects his son, Jack. Andrew has traveled the United States spreading the critical message about the need for increased funding for child brain cancer research. From a meeting with President Barack Obama in the White House Oval Office to numerous national media appearances on Fox News, CNN, ESPN, *ABC World News*, and *Good Morning America,* Andrew has provided leadership in the fight.

In the fall of 2012, the Hoffmans established the "Team Jack Foundation" (www.TeamJackFoundation.org) to further their efforts in the fight against childhood brain cancer. Since beginning his efforts at raising funds, he and his family have helped raise nearly eight million dollars and counting for pediatric brain cancer research via the Team Jack movement. Andrew has successfully lobbied and negotiated an additional three million dollars for co-funding for an over-eleven-million-dollar impact on disease research.

Andrew skillfully balanced his thriving law practice with his personal interest in helping kids. He has helped guide the recruitment and development of a full-time professional staff for Team Jack, including a skilled Executive Director, Kylie Dockter, so that he could continue his focus on his law practice. His primary role with the foundation is as Co-Board Chair with wife, Brianna.

Andrew always takes time to smell the roses. He is an outdoor enthusiast. He and his family enjoy walleye fishing, hunting, camping, and fixing fences on the family ranch.

Andrew was also an avid runner. His races have included the Boston Marathon (April 2014), the Los Angeles Marathon (March 2015, March 2020), the Chicago Marathon (October 2015), and the Minneapolis Marathon (2016 and 2017).

Andrew has been honored with The NASCAR Foundation's Betty Jane France Humanitarian Award in 2016, and in 2018, the "Hometown Hero Award," presented by FBI Omaha Division. Both awards reflect his work with the Team Jack Foundation.

To this day, Andrew remains passionate about pediatric brain cancer research funding. He will not stop until the day that he dies. He hopes this book will allow him to advocate beyond his life.